Paul Revere

and

Freemasonry

by
Edith J. Steblecki

Paul Revere and Freemasonry

All rights reserved.
Copyright © 1985 by Paul Revere Memorial Association

This book may not be reproduced in whole or in part, by mimeograph or any other means, without permission in writing.

Printed by Richter Associates, by arrangement with the copyright owners.

Cover description . . .

Mezzotint portrait of Paul Revere by Charles Balthazar Julian Fevret De Saint-Memin. Drawn with a "Physiognotrace," a mechanical device for tracing profiles, c. 1800. Courtesy, Paul Revere House.

Printed in the United States of America

TABLE OF CONTENTS

Preface	iii
Acknowledgements	iv
I. Freemasonry—A Definition	1
II. Organization and Ritual	4
III. St. Andrew's Lodge—The Early Years	10
IV. Founding a New Grand Lodge	20
V. The War Years	26
VI. Independence and Turmoil	36
VII. Enter Rising States Lodge	41
VIII. The Massachusetts Grand Lodge—Post War Decade	45
IX. Grand Master Paul Revere	52
X. George Washington—Death and Mourning	60
XI. Illustrations	*following page* 63
XII. Paul Revere—Masonic Decline	64
XIII. Exit Rising States Lodge	66
XIV. Paul Revere—Masonic Businessman	70
XV. Conclusion	76
Notes	79
Appendix 1	100
Appendix 2	102
Appendix 3	105
Appendix 4	107
Appendix 5	108
Selected Bibliography	120

PREFACE

Paul Revere, a well known historical figure, has been a familiar fixture of American folklore for many years. Not unlike other folk heroes, the fame of one event—in this case Revere's legendary "Midnight Ride" to Lexington—has served to obscure the facts of his productive and varied life. This study emerged from the desire to know more about Paul Revere's activities as a Freemason, thereby focusing attention upon a significant and fascinating aspect of the man and his world.

Although information on Paul Revere's masonic career does exist, this work attempts to compile the relevant data into one place. Most of this data has been gathered from primary sources, such as masonic Lodge minutes, and documents written by or relating to Paul Revere and Freemasonry. Unfortunately, Revere himself wrote little on the subject and Lodge minutes are often devoid of description, but they do provide a glimpse into the nature and extent of Paul Revere's involvement in eighteenth century Freemasonry. Quoted material from primary sources included in this work retains the spelling and punctuation of the originals. References to money, expressed in both pounds and dollars, also appear as in the original sources.

To avoid possible confusion, I would also like to clarify the usage of certain terms. The eighteenth century Freemasons are referred to simply as "masons". This designation was frequently used in masonic writings of the time. Regarding Revere's Lodges, the present day Lodge of St. Andrew is referred to here by its eighteenth century title—that of "St. Andrew's Lodge." Likewise, since the current Grand Lodge of Masons in Massachusetts was known historically as the "Massachusetts Grand Lodge," that is the title used here. Based upon the available information, what follows is a chronological survey of Paul Revere's masonic career, written from a non-masonic point of view.

ACKNOWLEDGEMENTS

Grateful thanks must be extended to the following for their assistance in the preparation of this book. To the Grand Lodge of Masons in Massachusetts located in Boston, I am indebted to several persons. Roberta Hankamer, Librarian, offered aid in research as well as providing illustrations for my slide lecture on Paul Revere's masonic career. Robert P. Beach, Grand Secretary of the Grand Lodge of Masons, and his assistant Kathleen Y. Ruland, graciously provided access to, and permitted photography of, the Revere material in the Archives. Robert W. Williams III, Managing Editor of *Trowel*, the magazine of the Grand Lodge of Masons, kindly published a shortened version of this work which appeared in the Fall/Winter 1984 and Spring 1985 issues.

Other institutions have also been of invaluable assistance. I must thank the Museum of Our National Heritage in Lexington, Massachusetts for providing me with the opportunity to lecture on this topic at the museum on December 2, 1984. It is also a pleasure to acknowledge members of the Lodge of St. Andrew for their interest in, and support of, this project. Special thanks are due Benjamin A.G. Thorndike and Henry Streeter, officers of that Lodge, for permission to view a microfilm of early Lodge minutes, and for reviewing the manuscript. Thanks are also due to those staff members of State Street Bank and Trust Company who facilitated my work on the manuscript.

Last, I am indebted to those individuals who made possible the use of illustrations included in this book, and to Patricia Sullivan and William Fowler for editorial advice and assistance.

I

FREEMASONRY—A DEFINITION

Paul Revere's masonic career spanned fifty years of his adult life, from 1760 to approximately 1810. (See Illustration 1.) These were years marked by change, encompassing the American Revolution and the early years of the Republic. For Massachusetts Freemasonry, it was also a period of growth and turmoil, in which Paul Revere played a prominent role. Both as a founding member and frequent officeholder, he left his mark on three Boston Lodges—St. Andrew's Lodge, the Massachusetts Grand Lodge, and Rising States Lodge. An examination of Paul Revere's masonic experiences will illuminate not only the history of these three Boston Lodges, but also what it meant to be a Freemason in the eighteenth century and how it affected the lives of men such as Paul Revere.

Freemasonry was first organized in America less than two years before the birth of Paul Revere. On July 30, 1733, a small group of men met at the Bunch of Grapes Tavern in Boston and formed the first masonic Lodge in America, later known as St. John's Grand Lodge. Although interested men had been conducting informal masonic meetings in the colonies since at least 1720, it was not until 1733 that Henry Price traveled to England and received official sanction from the Grand Master of the Grand Lodge of England for the first Grand Lodge in America. Henry Price is considered to be the "Father of American Freemasonry" as he was appointed the first "Provincial Grand Master of New England and Dominions and territories thereunto belonging," with sole authority to charter other Lodges within his jurisdiction. Before the American Revolution, this Grand Lodge chartered Lodges in the American colonies, Canada, Dutch Guiana and the West Indies.[1]

Nineteen years later, in 1752, St. Andrew's Lodge was organized. It was the fifth Lodge established in Boston and the fourteenth in the new world. Its founding relates to a movement which began in England, where, by 1751, a group of dissenters split from the English Grand Lodge and formed their own rival Grand Lodge, calling themselves "Ancient" masons. One source of their discontent was the original *Book of Constitutions* published in England by 1723, which revised some of the existing rules and ceremonies. The dissenters accused the English Grand Lodge of being "Modern", claiming that the revised ritual deviated so much from the ancient landmarks of masonry that the practices were no longer traditional. This rift between "Ancient" and "Modern" Freemasonry was not reconciled in England until 1813. The men who formed St. Andrew's Lodge in 1752, and met informally at the Green Dragon Tavern in Boston, considered themselves to be Ancient masons. They finally received a charter from the Grand Lodge of Scotland, a Lodge which was sympathetic to the Ancient movement. The Scottish Grand Master, Sholto Charles Douglas, Lord Aberdour, granted a dispensation on St. Andrew's Day, November 30, 1756. From this date, St. Andrew's Lodge was born. Paul Revere was one of the first initiates in this new Lodge.[2]

Paul Revere joined an organization which had been in existence for several hundred years. The view that Revere and his contemporaries held of Freemasonry was expressed in a volume of constitutions and rituals compiled in the 1790s, which contained "all things necessary for the use of the fraternity." Revere was on the committee which compiled the volume. (See Illustration 6.) The committee described "present day" Freemasonry as "an institution for the promotion of the most extensive philanthropy, the most diffusive and disinterested benevolence and universal virtue." Eighteenth century Freemasonry had evolved a long way from its origins in the fourteenth century when masons were stoneworkers who cut, laid and set stone. Under the direction of a Master Mason, masons in the Middle Ages constructed cathedrals, castles and monasteries, usually in rural areas where masons' groups, or lodges, took the place of regular medieval craft guilds. After seven years of training, a mason was entered in a Lodge as an "Entered Apprentice," where after seven further years of instructions, he became a "Fellow of Craft." The most skilled master builders were "Master Masons." As early as 1356, a code of regulations was written in London for the craft. As in most trade guilds, the "secrets" of the craft were jealously guarded, and a ceremony of admission had already evolved by 1390. Traces of masonic symbolism and its moral precepts began to appear as early as 1425. Still, there is a large gap between the stoneworkers' lodges of the fourteenth century and the modern masonic organization devoted to benevolence and philanthropy that Paul Revere joined several centuries later.[3]

The transition to modern Freemasonry began in England in the seventeenth century. As early as 1619, the London Masons' Company established an organization for men who were not stonemasons by trade. These men were known as "Accepted" masons, and seem to have had some knowledge of the stonemason's craft. Since the growth of architecture as a distinct profession was only beginning in the seventeenth century, the emerging gentleman's interest in architecture may have prompted some men to join masons' lodges. Also significant was the changing nature of the medieval guilds themselves. By the seventeenth century, the workers' craft associations had been gradually transformed along with the changing economy of England, and many guilds, including the masons' lodges, had practically become social clubs for workers. The fact that masonic lodges did not remain social clubs can be credited to the individuals who took an interest in the organization by the early eighteenth century.[4]

These men, heirs of the scientific revolution, were interested in science, philosophy and history. They saw in the traditions of Freemasonry the fraternity's potential as an agent of moral instruction. By imbuing the ancient rituals and traditions of the mason's craft with a higher moral tone, these men formulated an organization that provided a sense of social order, encouraged stable values, offered a hierarchy of merit within which members could attain status through instruction, while also instilling a universalism that transcended both political and religious diversity. It was a new sort of voluntary association, responsive to the anxieties created by the rapid social changes of the day. The establishment of modern Freemasonry was not without conflict, but the appealing organization persisted. In combining the conviviality of a social club with a sense of higher purpose, Freemasonry attracted men from all walks of life.[5]

This Freemasonic organization devoted to virtue, philanthropy, and benevolence took nearly two hundred years to develop completely. It was officially established in 1717, the year the Grand Lodge of England was founded. As early as 1735, masonic ritual, with its symbolic moral system based upon the mason's trade, was in full bloom in England. Since many men joining the fraternity were not working stonemasons, a distinction was needed. Non-stoneworkers had separate Lodges and were called "speculative" masons. These men came from all professions and, by the eighteenth century, probably had little actual connection with, or knowledge of, architecture and geometry. The actual working stonemasons were termed "operative". The volume of *Constitutions* compiled in 1792 explained the distinction.

> Formerly masonry was chiefly operative; confined to manual labor, and studied for improvement in those useful and elegant arts . . . But as morals, learning and religion advanced in the world, it became speculative, and attended to the cultivation of the mind, and the regulation of the manners . . .

Operative masonry referred to "the useful rules of architecture, whence a structure derives figure, strength and beauty . . ." while speculative masons "learn to subdue the passions . . . keep a tongue of good report, maintain secrecy and practice charity. . ." It was this sort of speculative, theoretical masonic organization that Paul Revere joined in 1760.[6]

II

ORGANIZATION AND RITUAL

Masonic ritual was solidly based not only on the mason's craft, but also upon religious symbolism. Much masonic ritual was built around the ancient biblical account of the building of King Solomon's Temple, a symbol which links the rituals of speculative masonry to their operative origins. The Temple appeared as part of the mythical history of Freemasonry as early as 1425. The practices and tools of the stonemason's craft were also imbued with symbolic religious and moral significance. Speculative masonry was "so interwoven with religion" that a man who was a mason would never be "a stupid *ATHEIST*" or "an irreligious *LIBERTINE.*" God was considered to be the "Glorious Master Builder of the Universe," as Jesus was the "*Chief cornerstone* of the Christian Profession." The feasts of St. John the Baptist and St. John the Evangelist were celebrated as summer and winter festivals following the early Christian traditions. Piety toward God and love to mankind were the "two grand immovable pillars" which held the whole structure together. The Bible itself was an important masonic symbol. A masonic Lodge could not legally conduct business without one, and every mason was "bound to be a strict observer of the moral law, as contained in the holy writings . . ." This pseudo-religious orientation of Freemasonary deliberately encouraged values that were universal to all faiths, thereby accommodating the religious diversity that was so widespread by the eighteenth century. Characteristic of the religious liberalism of that era, particularly the tendency toward deism, masons were not bound to any particular religion. They were required only "to be good men and true, or men of honor and honesty, by whatever denominations or persuasions they may be distinguished . . ." They were even advised to leave "their particular opinions to themselves," proclaiming only "that religion in which all men agree."[7]

Bound to rituals and practices centuries old, the eighteenth century masons were devoted to tradition, and keenly aware of their place in world history. With an Enlightenment faith in reason and harmony, they sincerely believed that their organization could have a positive impact on mankind. Masons were impressed with the universality of

Freemasonry, a belief which was evident in an address delivered by John Ward Gurley in 1800. Gurley proclaimed that the "eternal laws" of Freemasonry were seen to "pervade the universe," possessing a "moral system recognized in every region of the globe." With this moral system, according to the 1792 *Constitutions*, masons hoped to banish "Ignorance, superstition and vice . . . from the world." The process of changing the world began with individuals, and the masons knew that their personal conduct must be above reproach. At one meeting in 1784, St. Andrew's Lodge even warned the masons about the "ignorant and unenlightened" whose attempts to discredit Freemasonry had been " . . . constant and invariable for *AGES*." This desire to instill moral behavior and protect the reputation of Freemasonry is a recurrent theme in masonic writings. The public image of Freemasonry was also stressed in the *Constitutions*, where proper behavior was encouraged so that "all may see the benign influence of masonry, as all true masons have done from the beginning of the world and will do to the end of time." Masons exhibiting undesirable behavior were quickly fined or expelled, so as not to tarnish the reputation of the society as a whole. The minutes of St. Andrew's Lodge on May 2, 1780 mention one such individual who was "guilty of crimes the most atrocious." Through his actions, he caused "*Disgrace*, not only to *Masons* but the world of mankind." His name was swiftly "blotted out of the books."[8]

The "excellent moral system" which directed the lives of eighteenth century masons was based upon brotherly love: the "foundation and capestone, the cement and glory of this ancient fraternity." Masonic ceremonies, addresses, lectures and songs all reinforced the moral code. John Ward Gurley's address, delivered in Boston in 1800, described masonry as "a fabric designed by wisdom, reared by strength and decorated by beauty . . ." Although masonry was not open to women, Hannah Mather Crocker, a North End neighbor of Paul Revere, investigated the principles of Freemasonry in the late eighteenth century and found that " . . . the foundation is good, the chief Cornerstone is well laid with *wisdom, strength* and *Beauty* and ought to be adorned with *honour, Truth and justice* . . ." Qualities encouraged by a masonic sermon in 1796 include wisdom, patience, innocence, mildness, harmlessness and circumspection. These moralities "are the acknowledged appropriate articles of every Mason's Creed." The masonic message was transmitted through the public celebration of feast days, processions, lectures and funerals. The son of a recently deceased mason wrote a "heartfelt" letter of gratitude to Grand Master Paul Revere in 1795. He was impressed with the "fraternal respect" shown by the masons at his father's funeral, and professed his firm belief in masonry "on its true principles—philanthropy its basis; charity and benevolence its practice . . ."[9]

Benevolence and charity were encouraged "above all other virtues" as "the most distinguishing characteristicks" of Freemasonry, serving to enhance its reputation and appeal. Hannah Mather Crocker observed masonry to be "a society formed for the most benevolent purposes of charity." For masons themselves, the "principal advantage derived to society from the masonic institution is the encouragement and extension of its benevolent and charitable principles." Masons were encouraged towards "that liberal bestowment of alms" through which they would experience the "inconceivable pleasure of contributing toward the relief of our fellow creatures." With several notable exceptions, one being the masonic donation of £250 to the Boston Overseers of the Poor in 1777, masonic charity was principally confined to relatives, friends and neighbors of fellow masons.[10]

Examples of masonic charity dot the Lodge minutes, usually in the form of petitions for relief. Most references to charity involved passing the hat, such as when "a petition from Brother Phillip Bass was presented, and it was voted the hat should go round for his relief. There was gathered 28/." Wives and widows of masons "in distressed circumstances" were frequent petitioners, such as Mary, the wife of Brother Pulsifer. She was voted six pounds "out of the Lodge stock." It is not clear why the hat was passed for some cases, while others were assessed relief from the Lodge funds, but Lodges regularly accepted contributions for charity from prosperous masons. In 1779, Brothers Deval and Nottage donated $60 and $110 respectively to St. Andrew's Lodge for "the use of charity." By at least 1811, it was a regulation in many Lodges that the initiation fees be appropriated to the Charity Fund. The quarterly fees, or quarterages, due from members four times per year, also contributed to the Lodge's stock. Through the quarterages "every initiate thereby contributes to that stock from which he is entitled to relief in the day of adversity." It was the eighteenth century equivalent of Social Security.[11]

Masonic charity was not limited only to friends and acquaintances. Mark McCall, a "distressed Brother," petitioned St. Andrew's Lodge in 1778 for a "sufficient sum of money by which means he might be enabled to proceed to Philadelphia his place of residence." The petition was referred to a committee, as were many requests for relief. Masonic funds were not dispensed lightly. The *Constitutions* of 1792 did encourage charity to "strange brothers," but masons were not obliged to give beyond their ability. It was hoped that they would "prefer a poor brother, that is a good man and true, before any other person in the same circumstances." The following resolution from St. Andrew's Lodge suggests that, at times, masonic charity may have been a bit too generous, or perhaps the Lodge felt that it was losing control over the dispensation of funds. In 1783, the Lodge voted that:

> For the future, no sum or sums of money shall be paid by St. Andrews Lodge to any member or members who shall advance any

money to any person or persons who shall apply to them for Charity out of the Lodge.[12]

The ideals of Freemasonry were perpetuated by carefully approved members. According to the 1792 *Constitutions*, "the persons admitted members of a Lodge must be good and true men, free born, and of mature and discreet age, no Bondmen, no Women, no immoral or scandalous Men, but of good report." Although any freeborn male was eligible, Freemasonry was basically a closed society. Masons could propose candidates, but only with the approval of the Lodge Master. Once proposed, a candidate needed the unanimous vote of the Lodge members in order to gain admittance. Masons were even advised that

> If ever, in the circle of your acquaintances, you may find one desirous of being accepted among masons, you are to be particularly attentive not to recommend him, unless you are convinced he will conform to our rules . . .[13]

Guarding the sacred rules and "mysteries" of the order claimed a high priority among masons. Masonic secrecy and the availability of hidden knowledge were among the features which attracted men to masonry. Although many of the society's activities were public, members were sworn "never to communicate to your family, friends or acquaintances the private transactions and concerns of the Lodge." Masons were also directed to "be cautious in your words and carriage, that the most penetrating stranger shall not be able to discover or find out what is not proper to be intimated . . ." Members who disclosed the transactions of the Lodge were first publically admonished by the Master and later fined for repeated offenses.[14]

Technically, candidates were "entrusted with the secrets of masonry" if they were men of good character. Captain Robert Allen was granted admission because he was "a man with a Commission in the Army of the United States and consequently in the Character of a Gentleman." Once admitted as masons, members' behavior was monitored both in and out of the Lodge. The early bylaws of St. Andrew's Lodge, which were signed by Paul Revere, forbade cursing and swearing. No brother could enter the Lodge "diguised in liquor," nor would he be permitted to disrupt the "Harmony of the Lodge," where a "profound silence" was expected to be observed when the Master struck upon the table. No brother was permitted to interrupt while another was speaking, and "private piques and quarrels" were forbidden to be brought into the Lodge. Most of these offenses carried a small fine. Masons were also eager to avoid any disreputable behavior. Robert Fairservice, Jr. was "excluded from Visiting this Lodge [St. Andrew's] for a charge brot against him, till such time as it may appear the charge is false." The bylaws of St. Andrew's Lodge also forbade quarrels, fighting and abusive language in the Lodge room after the meeting was adjourned, since such behavior might cause the society to be "censured or reflected on and consequently liable to the aspersions and Contempt of the world . . ." Excessive gaiety after Lodge meetings was equally undesirable. Masons were directed to "avoid excess" and enjoy themselves with "innocent mirth." It is likely that there were "some irregular members" such as those described by a young potential mason in 1810. He recorded that " . . . it staggers my faith when I see many members sally forth after the Lodge is closed, in a very imprudent way. It makes me have my fears, of the effects it will have on the morals." Hannah Mather Crocker recognized that "the chief danger is from so large a number uniting in one social band of friendship" since "some of your jolly souls may take the advantage of being assembled to carry their mirth to an unreasonable degree." The desire to "avoid excess" and regulate proper behavior began early in St. Andrew's Lodge. In 1766, the Lodge even voted that "there be no stamping with the foot," while in 1769, it was "voted unanimously that Huzza be omitted for the future except on Feast Days." The masons must have found these expressions of enthusiasm undesirable if they chose to regulate against them.[15]

Although attracted by the purposes and ideals of the society, many masons probably appreciated the "social band of friendship" found in the fraternity. Attending St. John feast day festivals and Lodge meetings offered considerable recreation and a useful diversion from daily life. Hannah Mather Crocker compared masonry to "any other society formed for social intercourse." Masonic meetings were often held in taverns, the common meeting place for men in the eighteenth century. St. John's Lodge met at the Bunch of Grapes Tavern, while St. Andrew's met at the Green Dragon Tavern. Wine and rum were served on a regular basis, although not until after the business of the Lodge was over and the members were called to "refreshment". In St. Andrew's Lodge, smoking was not permitted until this point in the meeting. There were two Lodge Stewards, whose responsibility it was to provide "wine, rum lemons, etc. and take care of the same" and also to "keep the keys of the store closets, and see to drawing all the liquors." Often, a committee was appointed to assist the Lodge Stewards in purchasing rum and liquors for the use of the Lodge, particularly when planning feast day celebrations. The Feast of St. John the Evangelist, celebrated December 27, 1773, occasioned the consumption of fifty dinners, twelve bottles of Port and seventeen bottles of Madeira. In June 1772, the Feast of St. John the Baptist was attended by ninety-seven masons who consumed eleven bottles of Port, thirty-nine bottles of "Medaria" and thirty-four bowls of punch while they "dined together in the garden, under a long tent erected for that purpose; and the remainder of the day was dedicated to mirth and social festivity."[16]

Masonic Lodges regularly met one evening each month, usually from 6 to 10 in the summer and 5 to 9 in the winter. With feast days, funerals and other special occasions, meetings were often held with greater frequency. Paul Revere met with St. Andrew's Lodge on the second Thursday of the month. As a Master Mason, he also attended the St. Andrew's Masters' Lodge, which met quarterly on the fourth Thursday of February, May, August, and November. When the Massachusetts Grand Lodge was organized in 1769, Paul Revere was an active member. It met on the first Friday of March, June, September and December. After 1769, Paul Revere was also a member of St. Andrew's Royal Arch Chapter. At the very least, he spent no fewer than three or four evenings each month in masonic meetings. Hannah Mather Crocker first examined the principles of Freemasonry in order to "quiet the minds of several of my female friends, who were very anxious, on account of their husbands joining a Lodge. . ." The women were concerned about their husbands becoming Masons "lest it should injure their moral and religious sentiments," but also because "the hour of their retiring to rest was much later than usual, and infringed on domestick quiet and happiness." If Paul Revere's family life was seriously disrupted by his masonic activities, the record has not survived.[17]

III

ST. ANDREW'S LODGE—THE EARLY YEARS

At the age of twenty-five, on September 9, 1760, Paul Revere was initiated as an Entered Apprentice in St. Andrew's Lodge, receiving the first of three masonic degrees. The degrees were based upon the actual stoneworker's training, where masons advanced from apprentices to masters. On January 8, 1761, Paul Revere was "passed" to the Fellow-Craft degree, earning the highest degree, that of a Master Mason, only two weeks later on January 27, 1761. In the late eighteenth century, most men initiated in a Lodge advanced through the three degrees fairly rapidly, as did Revere. According to the early regulations of St. Andrew's Lodge, members were encouraged to advance, as any member who remained an Entered Apprentice for too long would "in due time be desird to withdraw unless he desires to be made a Fellow Craft." Through the three degrees, initiates were taught the basic truths and symbols of the craft, which acquired deeper meanings as they advanced toward the "sublime degree of Master Mason." After attaining the Master Mason degree, members might choose to examine masonic traditions in more detail or gain further distinction by serving as Lodge officers. Paul Revere did both. Just as election was based upon character, so advancement depended entirely upon merit. The 1792 *Constitutions* specified that "all preferment among masons is grounded upon real worth and personal merit only." Individual mobility was virtually limitless.[18]

No one knows what prompted Paul Revere to become a Freemason. Perhaps he noted the many prominent Bostonians who were members of St. John's Lodge, or chanced to see one of their masonic processions as a youth. At the impressionable age of twenty-one, Paul Revere joined the expedition against the French fort at Crown Point, New York—his only participation in the French and Indian War. He served as a second lieutenant of the artillery train in the regiment of Richard Gridley. Gridley was a mason and his regiment received a charter from St. John's Grand Lodge for an Army Lodge named Lake George, dated May 13, 1756. Revere served in the Crown Point expedition from February until late November and probably gained his first real exposure to Freemasonry. He must have liked what he saw, since his involvement with St. Andrew's Lodge followed shortly thereafter.[19]

If Paul Revere was inspired by his military experiences to join a Lodge, St. Andrew's was a logical choice. Many of its members lived and worked in his native North End. A list of members from early 1762 reveals the maritime orientation of the Lodge. (See Appendix 1.) Of the fifty-three members listed, there were eighteen ship captains, two sailmakers, a shipwright, a ship chandler and a ship joiner. Boat builder Nathaniel Hichborn, a cousin and later neighbor of Paul Revere, was also a member. Masons lived on Clark's Wharf, Pulling's Wharf and by Hallowell's shipyard. Paul Revere was only one of six fellow masons who lived on Fish Street. Others resided on Salutation Alley, Cross Street, and Middle Street, all in the North End. Of the fifty-three members, only seven were merchants. The remainder were artisans like Paul Revere, making their livelihood as gunsmiths, painters, bakers, carvers, and sugar refiners, to name a few. Revere might have felt more at home in this artisans' Lodge, rather than in St. John's Lodge, whose membership was slightly more elite.[20]

Unlike St. John's Lodge, St. Andrew's was a relatively new Lodge where an ambitious man could easily make his mark. Paul Revere was the Lodge's first legitimate initiate. Although the charter for St. Andrew's Lodge was issued in Scotland in 1756, it took four years for the document to cross the ocean. It was not until September 4, 1760 that the charter was finally laid before the Lodge. At the same meeting, Paul Revere was "made an Entered printiss," receiving the first degree. Nathaniel Hichborn followed close behind, being initiated by January 8, 1761. Robert Hichborn joined his brother and cousin in the Lodge on June 14, 1764. Paul Revere's devoted friendship with Joseph Warren also began in St. Andrew's Lodge. The young physician was initiated September 10, 1761, almost one year after Paul Revere.[21]

Tradition has it that St. Andrew's Lodge was first organized in the "Long Room" of the Green Dragon Tavern, a hall in the northerly end of the building, later famous for political meetings during the Revolutionary War era. (See Illustration 2.) The Lodge, in fact, had many homes in its early years. Several meetings in 1757 were held at Whateley's Inn. In 1760 and 1761, feast day celebrations were held in the Royal Exchange Tavern and the British Coffee House on King Street, and at the Greyhound Inn in Roxbury. Meetings of St. Andrew's Masters' Lodge from 1762 to 1764 may have been held at the homes of members. It was not until 1764 that St. Andrew's Lodge secured a permanent home owing to "the many Inconveniences they Labour under" with respect to the "place where they at present meet." On January 12, 1764, the members voted "to Purchase a House."[22]

By March 31, 1764, St. Andrew's Lodge purchased the Green Dragon Tavern from Catherine Kerr for £466 13s. 4d. Built of brick approximately 1680, the Tavern was located on the left side of Union Street, then Green Dragon lane, near the corner of Hanover Street. From the front, the building appeared to have two stories and a dormer floor, while in the rear, there were actually three stories with a basement. The attic floor was used for sleeping accommodations, the second floor contained the "Long Room," the largest meeting room in the northern end of town, and the lower story contained the tavern. Behind the building there were a stable and a garden, the property extending northerly to the Mill Pond. Leaving the old copper Green Dragon above the front door, the new proprietors added a large interlaced square and compass to the building's facade, this being the most prominent symbol of Freemasonry by the eighteenth century. The masons also renamed the tavern "Freemason's Arms" although it was changed to "Freemason's Hall" in June 1764, and then commonly shortened to "Mason's Hall." Old names die hard, and public announcements continued to list both names, even as late as 1773.[23]

The purchase of the Green Dragon Tavern was a process which involved many members of St. Andrew's Lodge, including Paul Revere, and lasted for thirteen years. Eight masons actually purchased the Tavern "in their own Names (but for the use of this Loge)." Thomas Milliken, one of the eight purchasers, probably acted as the proprietor, since the first few Lodge meetings were noted as being "held at Brother Milliken, Green Dragon Tavern." The Lodge held its first meeting at the Tavern on April 13, 1764, while repairs were still being made. Needed work was done by Lodge members, such as Thomas Crafts, a japanner and painter, who was paid £6 13s. 4d. on October 12, 1764 for "Painting the Floor Cloth." Three months later, on January 7, 1765, a bill was paid for "rebuilding Green Dragon Stable £26 6s 11d lawful money." Thomas Milliken, a bricklayer by trade, may also have done work on the Tavern, as he offered his bill, on March 27, 1766, of "£95. 14s. 4d. for repairs on Green Dragon after purchase."[24]

In the months following the purchase of the Tavern, committees continued to deal with the "affairs of the House." Although Paul Revere was not one of the eight original purchasers, he was chosen on May 10, 1764 "to joyn the Committee that Bought the House known by the name of the Green Dragon to Covennant with Rt. Wor. Burbeck." William Burbeck, a carver by trade, was Master of St. Andrew's Lodge when the Tavern was purchased. In the next several years, it seems that paying for the Tavern was an active concern among the masons of St. Andrew's Lodge. As early as October 12, 1764, £100 was "Paid to the Committee out of the Lodge's stock towards Masons Hall." By July 9, 1767, the Lodge decided to consult with James Otis, a prominent Boston lawyer, about the affairs of the House and paid him one guinea to attend a "Special Lodge" held the following evening. After meeting with Otis, the Lodge voted "that the affairs of this House be left under the Consideration of Mr. Otis until next Lodge Night." The

Lodge also voted that the Secretary "draw every B^r Acco^t: of what money they have paid towards the payment of this House."[25]

The affairs discussed with James Otis culminated in the following resolve. On February 11, 1768, it was

> Voted that the Standing Committee be desired to convey to the Right Worship" Brother Willm Burbeck the House commonly known by the name of Mason Hall upon his paying all the debts due from the Lodge of St. Andrew and also giving *Legal* security to such persons as said Loge shall appoint that upon there paying to the said Willm Burbeck the sum which he shall pay as aforesaid with lawfull Intrest then he shall reconvey to them the aforesaid House for the Use of St. Andrew Loge.

The arrangements were further discussed at a meeting held February 18, 1768. The eight masons who originally purchased the Tavern in 1764 were directed to convey the property to William Burbeck, who would then "give good security" to another group of seven masons, including only two of the original purchasers. These masons were then responsible for repaying Burbeck all that was owed to him, plus interest, within ten years. It was also voted at this meeting that "the sum to be received from B^r Burbeck be four Hundred Pounds LM°." After Burbeck was reimbursed, he would then "reconvey the said House, Land and premises free from all Incumbrances" to a group of seven other masons. This last group of seven included Paul Revere. The Lodge must have been satisfied with these arrangements since one month later, on March 10, 1768, the masons "voted unanimously that the whole transaction of the committee in the affairs of the House is quite agreeable," offering their thanks for the "good services in the affairs of the House."[26]

Despite this satisfaction, problems surfaced within the next few years. In April of 1771, a dispute arose with William Burbeck concerning the charter of St. Andrew's Lodge, which he held in his possession and refused to give up. Although there was no direct connection drawn in the Lodge minutes between this incident and the Tavern's purchase, a committee was also raised, at the same time, "to see in what manner the money for the House can be rais'd." This committee which consisted of five members included Paul Revere. The difficulties with the charter continued. In July 1772, Revere was one of a committee of three instructed to "warn Mr Burdick out this House." In April 1773, a Special Lodge was held which voted to "demand of Bro: Burbeck the Charter in his possession." When he gave no reply, the Lodge applied for a dispensation "to Hold and Continue this Lodge as usual untill their Charter is Received from the Grand Lodge of Scotland." Paul Revere was included on the committee selected to write to Scotland. At the same meeting, on May 13,

1773, William Burbeck was suspended. It was also voted that the Master of the Lodge must deposit the charter "on the Table Every Lodge Night," no doubt to guard against any future absences of the document.[27]

The settlement with William Burbeck for the Tavern, due within ten years, began drawing to a close in 1774. On February 10 of that year, a committee of five, including Paul Revere, was "appointed to see what Money they can procure from the members of this Lodge to pay off B. Burbeck for what is due to him on the house." By December 1776, Burbeck was again in favor with the Lodge, and the matter of the Tavern was finally concluded one year later on December 15, 1777, when it was "Voted Unan^y That B^r Burbeck reconvey the House to the five surviving Brethren of the Stand^g Committee," one of whom was Paul Revere. These five masons then conveyed the House to another committee of nine masons appointed for that purpose.[28]

While the legality of ownership was being determined, the Tavern underwent periodic repairs. Aside from initial repairs done after the building's purchase in 1764, little seems to have been done until 1768. Following the meeting with James Otis and the settlement with William Burbeck in 1768, it was voted that the "Standing Committee shall not do anything respecting the repairs of the House without first laying it before the Lodge for their approbation." Work began in May, two months later, when it was voted that "the roof of the House and Barn and the steps of the summer House and the Arch" should be repaired. By mid July, the Standing Committee discussed digging a new well, although the following month the Lodge voted "to clean the well that belongs to this House." By October 1768, it was voted to whitewash the lower part of the House and "gitt the Hall finished." Four years later, the building was still in need of repair when a meeting was adjourned "by reason of the Room being overflowed with Watter from the Late Storms." Not surprisingly, a motion was carried requesting the Standing Committee to "visit the House + see what Repairs is necessary to be done + Cause the same to be repaired." The same request was made by the Committee in June 1773, almost one year later.[29]

While the Lodge bore the expense of paying for the Tavern and its repairs, it may have been receiving some income through renting the building. Although no reference is made to rent before 1767, by June of that year the Standing Committee voted to raise the rent of the house to £75 or to "secure the use of the Hall solely for the Use of this Lodge." It appears that the Lodge continued renting the Hall. In 1780, the House was let quarterly at a rent of £40, while a year later, the rent was fixed at £60 per annum. Despite mention of rents, use of the Hall by other groups was infrequently recorded. In 1781, Perfect Union Lodge was given "liberty" to meet in Masons' Hall "on any evening except on the meeting of St. Andrew's Lodge." The Massachusetts Charitable Society was also obliged with the use of the Hall a year later. No rent is mentioned in either case. Likewise, on November 30, 1768, the use of the Hall was given to the Regimental Lodges of the Twenty-Ninth and Sixty-Fourth Regiments. It was also voted, in January 1769, to grant the "officers and Soldiers belonging to the Train of Artillery . . . the Liberty of this Hall to Exercise in ." They met with a Lodge member "giving security for making the hall good." The British soldiers had first arrived in Boston only two months earlier when Paul Revere wrote that "on Friday, September 30, 1768, the ships of war arrived. Schooners, Transports, etc, came up the harbour and anchored round the Town." There were many masons among the soldiers, to whom fraternal friendship was extended. The "Band of the British Troops" even supplied the music at the installation of Grand Master John Rowe for St. John's Grand Lodge on November 23, 1768. It was the Twenty-Ninth Regiment which would be involved in the "Boston Massacre" not two years later.[30]

Before the purchase of the Green Dragon Tavern in 1764, St. Andrew's Lodge spent its first years procuring Lodge necessities, setting policy and obtaining a charter. Although the Lodge was created by 1756, it was still in its formative years in the early 1760s, enabling Paul Revere to witness and participate in many Lodge "firsts", even after his initiation in 1760. The charter itself was not even received from Scotland until that year. A box was procured for its storage in July and a letter of thanks written to the Scottish Grand Master in September. After receiving the charter, bylaws were needed. St. Andrew's Lodge finished writing its bylaws by December 1760, using the bylaws of the "Lodge at Halafax N° 2" as a model. Necessary regalia were also procured in the early 1760s. The Lodge did not vote to obtain jewels until July 1760, these being the symbolic emblems worn by each officer of the Lodge. (See Illustration 3.) The Lodge also voted "that a Seal be provided" on February 12, 1761. Other Lodge furnishings came later, such as the "Genteel Chair" for the Lodge Master which was voted in November 1762, to be "paid for out of the Lodge stock." St. Andrew's Lodge also acquired a pair of ladles, when Samuel Barrett purchased two "Silver Punch Ladles" with "wooding Handles" from Revere in November 1762. (See Appendix 5.) The ladles were engraved to the Lodge, which voted its thanks to "our Brother Samuel Barrett SW for his donation to the Lodge of Two Genteel Silver Ladles" on November 30, 1762. The first recorded instance of masonic charity occurred in February 1761, when £5.6s.8d. was given to Brother Black who had "been a Sufferer in the Late Fire when Fauniel was burnt." By the following month a committee had been formed which wrote regulations for charity and provided a book for charitable activities.[31]

The first feast day celebration also occurred in 1761, when St. Andrew's Lodge voted to hold the Feast of St. John the Baptist. The following "advertisement" appeared in the local press.

> This is to give notice to the Brethren of the Ancient + Hon Society of Free + Accepted Masons that the Feast of St. John the Baptist will be Celebrated by the Brethren of St. Andrews Lodge/held by Authority for the R^t Hon The Lord of Aberdour Grand Master of Great Britain on Wednesday the 24th of June at the Royal Exchange Tavern in Boston. Tickets to be had of Moses Deshon + Saml Pecke Esq. + Joseph Webb J^r.

The second feast day was that of St. John the Evangelist, observed on December 27. When the Lodge chose to celebrate these feast days, they were the major masonic social events of the year, often consisting of a procession, a sermon and a dinner for which tickets were sold. A third important day for St. Andrew's Lodge was November 30, the feast day of its patron Saint. Beginning with November 30, 1762, the Lodge voted that "St. Andrews Night" be "sett apart as a Grand Lodge Night to be held annually by the Lodge to Chuse officers."[32]

Although feast days and elections demanded attention, they occurred infrequently and represent only a portion of the activity regularly conducted at masonic meetings. The most persistent activity involved the initiation, passing and raising of candidates through the three degrees. Men were proposed as candidates or members at nearly every Lodge meeting. There was a difference between becoming a mason in a Lodge and being made a member of the Lodge. A man could become a member of a Lodge even if he did not take the three degrees in that Lodge. The regulations for earning degrees and gaining membership were detailed in the bylaws. The third degree may have been given in St. Andrew's Masters' Lodge, a separate Lodge which met apart from the regular meetings of St. Andrew's Lodge specifically to confer "the sublime Degree of Master Mason." On January 27, 1761, when Paul Revere received the third degree, it was voted that the Masters' Lodge should meet monthly on the first Thursday, at which meetings no more than three masons could be raised in a single evening. The bylaws of the Masters' Lodge were recorded on September 10, 1762 and bore Paul Revere's signature.[33]

The early minutes of St. Andrew's Lodge also reveal that a commitment of money, as well as time, was demanded of men wishing to join the Lodge. By November 30, 1762, approximately two years after Paul Revere earned the first degree, it was voted "for the Future that the Expence of making an Enterd Prentice be Three Pounds, Six shillings & Eight pence Lawful money." By 1778, the fee for earning the same degree was nine pounds. But the ability to pay was not the only criterion for admitting masonic candidates. Masons desiring membership in St. Andrew's Lodge also needed the unanimous vote of the Lodge members. When Paul Revere was initiated in 1760, the vote may even have been taken openly. This is suggested by a resolution two years later, in April 1762, when the Lodge "voted unanimously that those Persons who shall be propos'd in future to be members of this Lodge shall be balloted for in the Box." Although candidates were sufficiently scrutinized, it was not difficult to advance rapidly through the three degrees once accepted. Under special circumstances, masons could even advance more quickly than usual. Due to the maritime orientation of St. Andrew's Lodge, individuals who were "bound to sea" were frequently granted more than one degree at a time, or had a degree proposed and conferred in the same evening, disregarding the usual time lapses specified in the bylaws. Exceptions were also granted to men who needed to leave town for other than seafaring reasons.[34]

After his initiation in 1760, Paul Revere did not remain idle. With masonic offices within his grasp, he advanced steadily upward until he was elected Master of St. Andrew's Lodge in 1770. The 1756 charter of St. Andrew's Lodge lists ten Lodge officers, ranked in the following order of seniority—the Master, Senior Warden, Junior Warden, Treasurer, Secretary, Senior Deacon, Junior Deacon and Tyler. There were also two Lodge Stewards. Several of the officers' jewels were based upon actual stonemasons' tools. Although a man could not be a Lodge Master until he had held other offices, advancement was determined by merit, rather than seniority. A man could not be a Master unless he was first a Warden, nor could he be a Warden until he was already a Master Mason. The Master presided over the Lodge. His jewel consisted of a square, a tool used for measuring right angles. The ideal Lodge Master was "nobly born, or a gentleman of the best fashion, or some eminent scholar, or some curious architect, or other artist, descended of honest parents and who is of singular great merit. . ." The Senior and Junior Wardens wore jewels bearing a level and plumb, respectively. The Senior Warden was essential, as he assisted the Master in Lodge business and governed the Lodge in the Master's absence. The Junior Warden was directed to "take care of the Reckening," a fee which each member paid at every Lodge meeting, as well as being responsible for the examination of visitors and the introduction of candidates. The Secretary kept two books, one containing a copy of the charter, bylaws and the list of members with the dates of their degrees, while the other book preserved the minutes of the meetings. The Secretary also issued summonses for meetings, and appropriately wore a jewel composed of two crossed quills. The Treasurer, whose jewel featured crossed keys, kept the Lodge accounts, while the Stewards helped with the feasts, attended to the Lodge refreshment, and accommodated visitors. In so doing, the Stewards' jewels bore a Horn of Plenty. The Deacons were directed only "to assist in their proper office at the making or raising of any Brethren," referring to the conferment of degrees, for which they would be "equipt with their proper wands." The Deacon's jewel bore the square and compass. The Tyler was the only officer who was regularly paid for his services. He was a guardian of the Lodge, and wore a jewel bearing swords, which were often crossed. His responsibilities also included delivering summonses.[35]

Paul Revere's career as a masonic officeholder did not begin in St. Andrew's Lodge until 1762. Although he was initiated in 1760, he did not receive the third degree until January 1761, when it was already too late for him to hold an office for that year. With his usual diligence, Paul Revere spent his first year as a mason learning and observing. Although he was not selected for any committees during 1761, he was present at every Lodge meeting held that year except one. Despite the fact that masonic Lodges technically met only once every month, St. Andrew's Lodge held twenty-six meetings in 1761. While this number may have been excessive, it was not unusual for Lodges to meet more than twelve times each year, as St. Andrew's Lodge regularly did. By December 1761, Paul Revere received his first masonic office when he was chosen as Junior Deacon for the year 1762. While he was not elected the following year, he served as Junior Warden in 1764 and Senior Warden in 1765. He received his next office in 1767, that of Lodge Secretary, a position he held through 1768 and 1769. After one year out of office, Paul Revere was elected to the highest office in the Lodge, that of Lodge Master, in December 1770. (See Appendix 2.)[36]

As Paul Revere advanced through the masonic hierarchy, he frequently filled in for absent officers of higher rank, and occasionally served in Lodge positions during years when he was not an elected officer. Although he was the elected Junior Deacon in 1762, he performed the offices of Junior and Senior Warden at six meetings during that year. In 1764, while serving as Junior Warden, he also filled the Senior Warden's position at four meetings. In keeping with his position as Senior Warden in 1765, Paul Revere also served as Lodge Master during three meetings when the elected Master was absent. In 1763 and 1766, when Revere was not holding any office, he was requested several times to serve as Junior and Senior Warden, which he also did in 1767, when he functioned as an officer at five Lodge meetings.[37]

Judging by his frequent service as a Lodge officer, Paul Revere was an eager mason in the early years as he advanced toward the position of Lodge Master. He attended meetings with diligent regularity. Out of 185 meetings held by St. Andrew's Lodge between 1761 and 1771, he missed only sixteen. His reliable presence did not go unnoticed, as he was soon selected for committees. His first committee appointment came in June 1762, when he was chosen to "join the Stewards to prepare and agree for the Feast" of St. John the Baptist. He served on the same committee the following year, and assisted with the feasts held in 1764 and 1766. Paul Revere also did committee work dealing with masonic charity and funerals. In June 1768, Revere was one of three masons directed to "draw up some regulations for funerals." A second committee formed ten months later for the same purpose also included Revere. The funeral regulations written by this committee were accepted in May 1769, although by June, it was voted to reconsider the regulations and the committee went back to work. The Lodge also needed regulations for charity. The earliest rules were drawn up in 1761, but by February 1766, Revere was instructed with four fellow masons to "draw some new Regulations for Charity + a New Book be bought for the Same." The articles for charity were accepted in April. Once written and accepted, it was voted in August that the charity regulations be shown to Deputy Grand Master John Rowe from St. John's Grand Lodge. His approval came with a subscription to the Charity Fund in December 1766. In July 1769, Paul Revere was chosen for a committee to inquire into the circumstances of Widow Darracott, wife of a deceased mason. At that meeting, she was given £3.6s.8d, while in November, £8 was collected from the Lodge members to be delivered to her by the committee. It was only one of numerous instances of masonic charity recorded between 1760 and 1770.[38]

After several years as an active mason and officeholder, Paul Revere desired to examine masonic traditions in more depth. He did this through St. Andrew's Lodge Royal Arch Chapter, which was just being organized in the 1760s. On October 29, 1762, a letter was written from St. Andrew's Lodge to the Earl of Elgin, Grand Master in Scotland, "soliciting a Royal Arch Charter with power to form more lodges in America." Although a chapter was probably already meeting unofficially, the charter for the Royal Arch Chapter was not received until August 28, 1769 when, meeting in the "Long Room," St. Andrew's Chapter No. 1 was

> authorized to hold a charter of Royal Arch Masons and to exalt at their discretion any master mason to the Degree of Royal Arch Mason, and for that purpose to open and hold Lodges of Mark Masters, Past Masters and most excellent masters, agreeably to the ancient usages and customs of Royal Arch masons and also to make and establish any good and wholesome bylaws. . .

Paul Revere became a Royal Arch mason before the year was over. At the Royal Arch Lodge held in Masons' Hall on December 11, 1769, "a petition of Brother Paul Revere coming before the Lodge begging to become an Arch Mason it was red and he was unanimously accepted and accordingly made." Joseph Warren received the degree on May 14, 1770. There were only five Royal Arch initiates between 1770 and 1773.[39]

IV

FOUNDING A NEW GRAND LODGE

As St. Andrew's Lodge organized and expanded, the masons sorely desired the approval and fraternal respect of their fellow brethren in St. John's Grand Lodge. They failed to receive it. This conflict led directly to the founding of a new Grand Lodge in Boston. St. John's Grand Lodge, which was already held in Boston, claimed exclusive masonic authority in Massachusetts and refused to recognize St. Andrew's Lodge, particularly after St. Andrew's received a legitimate charter, as they "imagined their jurisdiction infringed by the Grand Lodge of Scotland." In February of 1761, St. Andrew's Lodge wrote to its Scottish Grand Master, noting the refusal of St. John's Lodge to admit visitors from St. Andrew's. It was a common practice for Freemasons to attend meetings of other Lodges as visitors, but St. John's would not allow this. St. John's Grand Lodge forbade the masons under its jurisdiction "to appear at the meeting (or the Lodge so called) of Scotts Masons in Boston, not being regularly constituted in the opinon of this (Grand) Lodge. . ." This vote of "outlawry against a Lodge [of] Scotch masons in Boston" was passed April 8, 1761. Two years later, in 1763, St. Andrew's Lodge was still writing to Scotland about the uncharitable position of St. John's Grand Lodge.[40]

The relationship between the two Lodges had not improved by 1766. The masons of St. Andrew's Lodge still sought masonic fraternity with their brethren in St. John's Grand Lodge, feeling that "harmony and sincere friendship are ornaments which add the greatest lustre to masonry." Toward this end, on January 22, 1766, St. Andrew's Lodge chose a committee to visit St. John's Lodge "with a complimentary address to Desire them to Visett this Lodge whenever they may think proper," hoping that "for the future there may be a happy coalition." The response from St. John's Lodge was anything but cordial. According to St. Andrew's Lodge, it was "by no means satisfactory as it is ill Grounded." The reply contained "a series of offensive votes" which labeled the members of St. Andrew's Lodge as "irregular masons" or worse, not masons at all. A meeting on May 2, 1766 between committees of both Lodges softened the controversy, and letters were sent to Scotland in June transmitting "all that past between the Grand Lodge of Boston and this Lodge [St. Andrew's]." The problem remained unresolved, however, and St. Andrew's Lodge felt the need to issue the following vote against St. John's in November 1767.

> Whereas the Grand Lodge held in Boston whereof the late Jer^r Gridley Esq was G^r. M^r. passed a vote that no Master or Masters of any Lodge under his jurisdiction more especially in Boston should not on any consideration admit of the visits of any of the Members of St. Andrews Lodge which vote is disadvantageous to this Lodge in as much as many Gentlemen have been thereby prevented from offering themselves to be made here. therefore Voted that this Lodge will not from henceforth admit of the Visits of the Members of any of the Lodges in this town or any person that shall be made therein untill the said Vote of said Grand Lodge shall be reconsidered and made Void Except they are members of this Lodge or have been Raised Master here.[41]

The undesirable relationship between the two Lodges failed to improve and by November 30, 1768, St. Andrew's Lodge considered "the expediency of applying to the Grand Lodge of Scotland for a Grand Master of Antient Masons" in America. This Ancient Grand Master would serve as a representative of the Scottish Grand Lodge, just as the Master of St. John's represented the Grand Lodge in England. Such a move would give St. Andrew's Lodge equal rank with the Modern masons of St. John's Grand Lodge. Paul Revere and Joseph Warren served on an eight man committee which consulted the other Ancient Lodges in Boston, these being three British military Lodges which had arrived in Boston nearly two months earlier. After meeting with the Lodges of the Sixty-Fourth, Twenty-Ninth and Fourteenth regiments, by December 8, 1768, the masons were "agreed that it is necessary to have a Grand Master of Antient Masons in America" and proceeded to propose officers for the new Lodge, after which St. Andrew's Lodge petitioned the Scottish Grand Master, Right Honorable George, Earl of Dalhousie, for a Provincial Grand Master. Under a commission dated May 30, 1769, Joseph Warren was installed as the "Grand Master of Masons in Boston, New England, and within one hundred miles of the same." The installation took place at Masons' Hall, December 27, 1769 in a public ceremony. Paul Revere was also installed as an officer. In September 1769, while still serving as Secretary of St. Andrew's Lodge, Revere had acknowledged "the receipt of the Grand Master's Commission" and accepted his position as Senior Grand Deacon of the new Grand Lodge of Ancient masons, also known as the Massachusetts Grand Lodge.[42]

Paul Revere was not the only mason from St. Andrew's Lodge to hold an office in the new Massachusetts Grand Lodge. Of the ten original officers, eight were active members of St. Andrew's Lodge.

The two Wardens, who were appointed from the military Lodges, participated little in Lodge affairs, and their appointment was largely a courtesy. They attended several meetings, the last being that of March 2, 1770, three days before the "Boston Massacre." Particularly in the beginning, the Massachusetts Grand Lodge was closely related to St. Andrew's Lodge. Aside from sharing many members, both Lodges met in Masons' Hall, with the Grand Lodge meeting quarterly on the first Fridays of March, June, September and December. In September 1769, St. Andrew's Lodge provided and financed the "Ribbons, Mallatts, Wands, etc." needed by the Grand Lodge. This arrangement must have been acceptable, since the Grand Lodge again asked St. Andrew's Lodge for "the use of their Room and Utensils" in October 1770. In December 1771, St. Andrew's Lodge acknowledged the gratitude of the Grand Lodge for "the use of the Utensils the year past" and unanimously voted for a continuance of their use. The new Grand Lodge also obtained its officers' jewels through St. Andrew's Lodge. In September 1769, St. Andrew's voted "that the Grand Lodge be provided with Jewells made of any mettal under silver, and that this Lodge accept of Brother Revere's offer to make the Jewells and wait for his pay till the Grand Lodge is in Cash to pay him." In December 1770, the Grand Lodge asked Senior Grand Deacon Paul Revere to cut a seal for the Lodge, for which he would be paid on account from "the money arising from the charters of the Massachusetts and Tyrian Lodge." There was always a fee charged when a Grand Lodge chartered Lodges under its jurisdiction. In this instance, it took Revere one year to get paid, as the Grand Lodge did not vote him payment until December 6, 1771. (See appendix 5.)[43]

For Paul Revere, these were busy years. Not only was he actively involved with two masonic Lodges, but he was also a member of the North End caucus. He had recently purchased a house on North Square, on February 15, 1770, where he moved with his wife Sara, his mother and five children. Another daughter would be born before the year was over. Along with being a devoted family man, Revere worked as a goldsmith, dabbled in dentistry and produced engravings, one of his most famous being the depiction of the Boston Massacre of March 5, 1770, produced shortly after he moved to North Square. As a Freemason, Paul Revere served the Massachusetts Grand Lodge as Senior Grand Deacon from December 1769 to 1774. Recall that he was also Master of St. Andrew's Lodge in 1771, being elected December 1770. As Master, Revere represented St. Andrew's Lodge at the Grand Lodge meetings, paying the appropriate charges and casting votes. He also acted in this capacity for Tyrian Lodge when, on October 14, 1770, "Brother Revere produced a deputation from the Tyrian Lodge appointing him their proxy which was read and Unanimously accepted." This empowered Revere to pay dues and cast votes for Tyrian Lodge, which was chartered in Gloucester on March 2, 1770.[44]

Chartering Lodges under its jurisdiction was one of the primary functions of the new Massachusetts Grand Lodge, which issued thirteen charters between 1770 and 1780. Tyrian Lodge was the first Lodge chartered, but others soon followed. Massachusetts Lodge, which was chartered May 13, 1770, was officially installed at Concert Hall on Friday evening August 10, where "the Evening concluded with that social festivity which becomes good Masons." In return, Lodges provided monetary support to the parent Grand Lodge at each quarterly meeting. On October 14, 1770, it was voted that the Lodge representatives pay twelve shillings at every quarterly communication. In December, Paul Revere "reported from St. Andrew's and the Tyrian Lodge that they agreed to send two doll^{rs} to the Grand Lodge." The Grand Lodge also received payment when new Lodges were chartered. Chartering a Lodge was a tedious process, usually involving an investigation into the characters of the petitioners which could last several months. Not every petition was approved, such as that of a group in Portsmouth, desiring to form a Lodge of St. John. On November 6, 1772,

> the Committee appointed by the Grand Lodge some months past to enquire into the characters of the foregoing petitioners, Report, that after strict enquiry, some of their characters appeared to be such, that they [the committee] could not reccommend them as worthy of a warrant.

It was also the duty of the Grand Lodge to see that new Lodges were properly organized. In 1772, Paul Revere served on a committee which conferred with a new Lodge in Newburyport. Along with investigating and chartering Lodges, the Grand Lodge elected officers for each year, planned and observed feast days, and collected dues.[45]

Theoretically, the Grand Lodge met quarterly—four times per year. In reality, at least in the early years, Lodge meetings were held with greater frequency. There were at least eight meetings in 1770, nine in 1772, seven in 1778 and six in 1773 and 1779. As a prominent officer throughout this period, having been chosen as Senior Grand Deacon from 1769, Paul Revere attended many more meetings than he missed. In December 1772, it was decided that the Grand Lodge officers should be elected annually on the first Lodge night in December, at which time Paul Revere was again chosen as Senior Grand Deacon, serving through 1774. For at least one meeting in 1774, Paul Revere was Grand Treasurer, as it was "motioned and seconded a Treasurer be chose. Voted Brother Revere be Grand Treasurer." By the next meeting, however, another mason was listed in the office. Paul Revere continued to hold offices in the Grand Lodge throughout the 1770s and early 1780s. (See Appendix 2.)[46]

As in St. Andrew's Lodge, Paul Revere took an active role in the Massachusetts Grand Lodge. He was frequently involved with planning for feast day celebrations. In preparation for the Feast of St. John the Baptist on June 24, 1772, Paul Revere was "joined with the Committee for preparing the music," having been absent from the previous meeting when the committee was first raised. This feast is fully described in the Lodge minutes. With ninety-seven people present, including Revere, the brethren

> Congregated at Eleven o'clock A.M. at Concert Hall where the Grand Lodge was open'd in ample Form, after which the Brethren . . . all cloath'd in their respective Jewells, and with their several badges of Office, marched in procession to Christs Church where a very suitable and pertinent discourse was preached by the Rev[d] Brother Samuel Fayerweather of Narragansett . . . after which the order of procession was reversed . . . and they march'd to Mason's Hall where the Grand Lodge again formed and . . . Voted Unanimously that the Thanks of this Lodge be given to the Rev[d] Dr. Byles Jun[r] for his performance of prayers this day and for his + the Church Wardens' + Vestry's granting us the Liberty of Assembling at Christs Church: Also to the several Gentlemen proprietors of pews there, for their ready consent in granting the sole use of their Pews for the purpose aforesaid . . . The Lodge was then closed, after which the Gd Master and Brethren dined together in the Garden, under a large tent erected for that purpose, and the remainder of the Day was dedicated to Mirth and Social Festivity.

Paul Revere, Joseph Webb and Thomas Crafts were appointed a committee to wait on the Reverend Fayerweather and request a copy of his sermon for the press, and also to thank the Reverend Byles, and the Wardens and Vestry of Christ Church. In September 1772, three months later, Paul Revere was one of a committee of three appointed "to examine how the several Sums collected for defraying the expence of the Festival of St. John the Baptist was disposed of."[47]

On December 4, 1777, when planning for the Feast of St. John the Evangelist, Revere and two others were directed to "Procure the Liberty of the Chaple (stone), also to Request of Col. Crafts, his Reg[t] Musick, and M[r] Silsby to perform the Organ Musick at the Chapel." The following year, for the same feast, Revere was one of a committee of three that approached the Reverend Mr. Howard about preaching the sermon. On December 18, "Bro Col Revere . . . Reports That the Rev. Mr. Howard will deliver a Sermon to the Body of Masons at the Old Brick Meeting [house]." On the feast day, December 28, 1778,

> The Brethren Marched, to the Old Brick Meeting House where the Revd M[r] Howard preached a Sermon . . . then Returned to the Hall,

and after Partaking of an Elegant Feast, Voted, the Thanks of the Grand Lodge be given to the Rev[d] Mr. Howard for his Sermon deliverd this day and that the following Brethren wait upon him, Return him thanks and Request a Copy of the Same for the Press . . .

Paul Revere was one of the five Brethren appointed for this purpose. Revere was also one of three masons who had been chosen on December 18 to see that "The Honbl General Gates, and such of his Family, who are Masons, be waited upon, + Invited to dine at the Feast." General Gates and his family did attend the Feast at Masons' Hall, along with 103 brethren of the Grand Lodge.[48]

V

THE WAR YEARS

Although every attempt was made to observe feasts, elect officers and conduct business as usual, the decade from 1770 to 1780 was marred by the commencement of hostilities between Great Britain and the American colonies. While the theatre of war had moved away from Boston by 1777, the conflict had a definite impact on Massachusetts Freemasonry, just as the masons had a definite impact on the war. Broadly speaking, the masons of St. Andrew's Lodge tended toward more radical views. They observed the Stamp Act Riots in 1765 with the destruction of Lieutenant Governor Thomas Hutchinson's mansion in the North End. They witnessed the arrival of British troops in 1768 and finally the so called "Boston Massacre" in 1770, the result of increasing tensions between citizens and soldiers that left five Americans dead. Masonic records are deceptively silent about current political discussions. In fact, the later masonic *Constitutions* of 1792 specifically forbade "quarrels about religion, or nations, or state policy. . . " Although it is likely that political discussions were not conducted during masonic meetings, there would be no barring such discussion after the Lodge was closed. Tradition has it that the masons of St. Andrew's Lodge were very much involved.[49]

While Paul Revere was busy holding masonic offices and helping to found the new Grand Lodge, tensions were rapidly increasing between America and the mother country. Beginning with the Stamp Act in 1765, the Townshend Duties in 1767 and the final tax on tea in 1770, Great Britain was determined that the colonists should bear some of the expense that the "French and Indian War," fought on American soil, had cost the British empire. To the King's ministry, taxation seemed a reasonable way to raise money, as well as help to support the small number of British troops stationed in America. It all seemed entirely unreasonable to the Americans, who countered with nonimportation of English goods, riots and occasionally violence. With the repeal of the Townshend Duties in 1770, a relative calm settled over Boston, finally erupting three years later over the Tea Tax at the "Boston Tea Party." The East India Act of 1773 was designed to assist the indebted British East India Company by selling its surplus tea on the American market at a very low price, thereby underselling the Dutch tea illegally smuggled into the American colonies. The lower prices would give the East India Company a virtual monopoly on tea in America, while supplying England with the duty on imported tea from the Tea Tax of 1770. Although seemingly advantageous to the colonists, in that it lowered tea prices, it was a thoroughly unpopular act.

In these troubling times, Paul Revere was no stranger to political meetings. He belonged to the North End Caucus, as well as being a member of the Long Room Club, one of the earliest radical groups in Boston. It was composed largely of scholarly men who met secretly in a room above the printing office of Edes and Gill, publishers of the *Boston Gazette*. Paul Revere advertised in the *Boston Gazette*, as did the Massachusetts Grand Lodge. Political groups had much to discuss while anticipating the arrival of the East India Company Tea in 1773. On the morning of Monday, November 29, 1773, the following announcement was posted calling Bostonians to meet:

> Friends Brethren Countrymen! That worst of Plagues, The Detestable Tea ship'd for this port by the East India Company is now arrived in this harbour. The Hour of Destruction or manly Opposition to the Machinations of Tyranny Stares you in the Face: every Friend to his Country, to himself and Posterity is now called upon to meet at Faneuill Hall at 9:00 this day (at which time the Bells will begin to ring) to make a United + Successful Resistance to this last, worst and most destructive Measure of Administration. Boston November 29, 1773.

Paul Revere was probably among the one thousand people who met at Fanueil Hall that day.[50]

According to traditions of the Lodge of St. Andrew, plans for the destruction of the tea were matured at the Green Dragon Tavern, involving many members of St. Andrew's Lodge and the North End Caucus. On November 30, 1773, the day following the Fanueil Hall meeting, St. Andrew's Lodge held its regular monthly meeting. It was also "St. Andrews Night," the evening of the annual election of officers, which was usually well attended. On this night, however, the attendance was meager and the Lodge minutes significantly recorded that the "Lodge be Adjourned to Thursday Evening Next, on account of the few Brethren present. (N.B. Consignees of Tea took up the Brethren's Time.)" Wishing to avoid paying the tea tax, the patriots demanded that the tea ships be permitted to return to England without unloading their cargo. This was impossible because once the ships passed Castle Island, they were technically within Boston Harbor and were required by law to pay the duty within a specified amount of time, or else the cargo could be seized by the customs officials. The seventeenth of December was the day when the cargo could be forcibly confiscated. Days of negotiations between the Governor, the tea merchants and the patriots produced few results. Finally, on December 16, 1773 "a number of people appearing in Indian dresses went on board the three ships . . . They opin'd the Hatches, hoisted out the Tea and flung it Overboard . . ." Although "near two thousand people were present," no attempt was made to stop the destruction.[51]

No list was preserved recording the identities of the "mohawks." Joseph Warren, Samuel Adams, John Hancock, Joseph Webb, Thomas Melville and Paul Revere are noted as having had knowledge of the event, if not actually participating themselves. On December 16, the day of the "Tea Party," the regular meeting of St. Andrew's Lodge was again poorly attended, with only five officers present. Paul Revere's name was not among them. The Lodge was "Closed (on account of the few Memberss present) untill tomorrow Evening." According to an account printed in 1870, the following members of St. Andrew's Lodge took an active role at the "Tea Party": Adam Collson, Thomas Chase, Samuel Gore, Daniel Ingollson, Samuel Peck, Edward Proctor, Henry Purkett and Thomas Urann. Although this list does not include Paul Revere, fragments survive of a song said to have been written for the "Tea Party" which mentions Revere specifically. A verse exclaims that "Our Warren's there and bold Revere, with hands to do and words to cheer for Liberty and Laws! Our country's 'Braves' and firm defenders, shall ne'er be left by true North-Enders, Fighting Freedom's cause!" Not all Freemasons were enthused about the "Tea Party." John Rowe, Master of St. John's Grand Lodge, wrote that the incident "might I believe have been prevented," adding "I am sincerely sorry for the event." On December 18, he wrote that "the affair of destroying the Tea makes Great Noise in the Town—tis a Disastrous affair and some people are much alarmed." He added "I can truly say, I know nothing of the matter nor who were concerned in it." While John Rowe lamented the effects of the incident, an undaunted Paul Revere was "employed by the Selectman of the Town of Boston to carry the Account of the Destruction of the Tea to New York." It was only one of many messages he carried during the revolutionary period.[52]

The "Tea Party" of December 1773 had serious repercussions in Boston by June of 1774. The Crown was determined that the colonies should be submissive to Parliament, and demanded that Boston pay for the lost tea. Parliament adopted four acts, known as the Coercive Acts, which were intended to discipline Massachusetts and serve as an example of royal authority to other colonies. News of the first act, the Boston Port Act, reached the city by early May 1774, declaring Boston Harbor blockaded and closed to all commerce until the colonists paid for the tea. The blockade went into effect June 1, 1774. The act disrupted Boston life, as well as its masonic Lodges. At a meeting of June 3, 1774, the Massachuetts Grand Lodge voted that "this Grand

Lodge be adjourned to Tuesday evening next 7 o'clock by reason of the few Grand Officers present, Engaged in Consequential Public Business." Whatever the business was, Paul Revere was probably involved, since he was not at Masons' Hall that night. Although the "Public Business" is not specified, it is not difficult to imagine the disruption created by the Coercive Acts in early June of 1774. Paul Revere was present at the meeting on June 7, when the Grand Lodge also voted not to hold the Feast of St. John on June 24, after which they declared "this Grand Lodge closed until the first Friday in September." On September 2, the Lodge adjourned because of the few people present. Although St. Andrew's Lodge still met throughout 1774, the Masters' Lodge did not meet from 1773 until 1777.[53]

By Fall 1774, Paul Revere was increasingly involved with radical activities. In his own words, he was employed by the Selectmen "to carry their dispatches to New-York and Philadelphia for Calling a Congress; and afterwards to Congress, several times." This activity out of town disrupted Revere's regular Lodge attendance, and he missed all but one meeting of St. Andrew's Lodge between August and December 1774. Paul Revere also carried the "Suffolk Resolves" to Congress, which had been written by Joseph Warren for a Suffolk County gathering held at Milton, Massachusetts. The Resolves declared that the Coercive Acts should not be obeyed and recommended a severance of trade with Great Britain. While the Resolves expressed the determination to act only on the defensive, they also encouraged Americans to be prepared for any British movements out of Boston. The Congress voted its approval of the Resolves on September 17, 1774, and Paul Revere returned to Boston.[54]

In accordance with Warren's Resolves, Paul Revere wrote that he soon became "one of upwards of thirty, chiefly mechanics, who formed our selves in to a Committee for the purpose of watching the Movements of the British Soldiers, and gaining every intelegence of the movements of the Tories." It is likely that several of the "mechanics" were also brethren from St. Andrew's Lodge, since Revere and his fellows "held our meetings at the Green Dragon Tavern." This continued from the Fall of 1774 until the Spring of 1775, during which time the committee "frequently took Turns, two and two, to Watch the Soldiers, By patroling the Streets all night."

This surviellance led to Paul Revere's famous midnight ride, when he and William Dawes carried the warning of a British expedition to Lexington on the night of April 18, 1775. With the first battle of the American Revolution, on April 19, 1775, masonic activity ceased. St. Andrew's Lodge minutes reveal no record of formal meeting for one year, from April 13, 1775 until April 18, 1776. The Massachusetts Grand Lodge noted on April 19 that "Hostellitys Commenc'd between the Troops of G. Britain and America, in Lexington Battle. In Consequence of which the Town was Blockaded and no Lodge held until Dec 1776."[55]

When the Lodges reconvened, the war still continued to leave its mark on masonic activities throughout the late 1770s. As early as February 24, 1776, plans were made by the British to use the Green Dragon Tavern as a hospital.

> Having occasion for a large Commodious House for the purpose of a hospital in which the poor—Infirm and Aged can be lodged . . . and having the consent of the Proprietors in Town of the House commonly called the Green Dragon to apply that to this purpose, you are hereby required to take possession of said House and prepare it as a Hospital for the Reception of such objects as shall require immediate Relief . . .

The Tavern was probably not a hospital for very long since the sudden appearance of George Washington's cannon atop nearby Dorchester Heights forced the British to evacuate Boston in March of 1776.[56]

The St. Andrew's Lodge minutes reveal numerous instances of masonic charity, most of which were related to relieving the hardships of war. In the winter of 1777, the members of St. Andrew's Lodge voted £250 for the Boston Overseers of the Poor. In February 1778, while Paul Revere was Lodge Master, a petition for relief

> in favor of our distressed Brother Moses Abraham Wallach (a Dutch Young Gentleman who was taken by one of Tyrant Georges Frigates & had everything taken from him even to his Certificate) was read . . . Voted Unanimously, That a committee be chosen to provide suitable Lodgings and a passage to some Dutch Island in the W. Indies . . . that there be a Collection this Evening to defray the neccessary Expences . . . and any defficiency made up by the Lodge and that the Sec^y present him a Certificate from this Lodge—Collected for the aforenamed B^r £18. 15.

Along with foreign brothers, the masons also assisted British prisoners of war. On February 17, 1778, £3 were given to a prisoner, Sergeant James Andrews, "as a Token of the Love and friendship this Society has for one of the Fraternity tho' an Enemy." In January 1779, the hat was sent round for a "native of Britain + a *distressed brother*" for whom £33 were collected. Similarly, in 1782, the hat was again passed "for distressed strange brethren." The Grand Lodge of Scotland gratefully thanked St. Andrew's for their "attention and kind offices to British brothers, prisoners of war."[57]

The Massachusetts Grand Lodge also assisted prisoners of war. On June 4, 1779, the Lodge voted

> . . . that the G^d Sec^y write to the Commissary of Prisoners, at Rutland, and know the rank of Richd Speaight and others who have petitioned this Grand Lodge, to use their influence with the Honorable Council to grant them a parole to go to New York—promising an Exchange of officers of Like Rank.

The Grand Lodge also contributed to the relief of the poor. The Feast of St. John, on December 28, 1778, was celebrated by the Grand Lodge with the usual masonic procession and sermon, after which "a collection was made for the Poor of this Town" and delivered to the Boston Overseers of the Poor. Two years later, again at the Feast of St. John the Evangelist, a "Handsome Collection was made for the Poor," after which the brethren "returned to the Hall and Enjoy'd themselves upon an Elegant Dinner provided to Honor + Respect the day." Another "Handsome Collection" was delivered to the Overseers of the Poor after the Feast of St. John the Baptist in June 1782. Masons themselves also experienced hardship during the war years. Contrary to the elegant dinners usually held on feast days, the Grand Lodge voted not to hold the Feast of St. John in December 1781, "on the Principle that the . . . prices are beyond the ability of many Brethren to Support, without Apparent Injury to their Families." Although general collections for the poor were taken most frequently during the war years, individual petitions for relief were often addressed at feast day celebrations when large numbers of brethren were assembled. In 1791, it was even voted that "the remains of the feast be sent to the prisoners in the Gaol."[58]

The conflict between England and her colonies dealt a serious blow to the Massachusetts Grand Lodge. During the Battle of Bunker Hill, on June 17, 1775, Grand Master Joseph Warren lost his life. Although he had been commissioned a Major General, he died fighting as a private soldier. He had served the Lodge as Grand Master for five and one-half years, with Paul Revere as his Senior Grand Deacon from 1769 until late 1774. The loss of Warren created a crisis for the Lodge, since, as Grand Master, he had been appointed by the Grand Lodge of Scotland. It was uncertain whether it would be legal simply to elect another Grand Master, or whether the Lodge would be forced to wait until the Scottish Grand Master appointed a new head. The problem was postponed until December 1776. In the interim, the Grand Lodge did not meet while the British still occupied Boston. When the British evacuated Boston on March 17, 1776, almost nine months after the Battle of Bunker Hill, several masons gathered "influenced by a pious regard to the memory of the late Grand Master . . . to search for his body which had been rudely and indiscriminately buried on the field of slaughter." The masons intended to give Joseph Warren a proper masonic funeral.[59]

Paul Revere was probably with the brethren who searched for Joesph Warren's body on March 18, 1776, a day which was described in masonic records, when the men

> accordingly, repaired to the place and by direction of a person who was on the ground about the time of his burial, a spot was found where the earth had been recently turned up. Upon removing the turf and opening the grave, which was on the brow of a hill, and

adjacent to a small cluster of sprigs, the remains were discovered in a mangled condition but were easily ascertained (*by an artificial tooth) and being decently raised were conveyed to the State House in this metropolis; from whence, by a large and respectable number of brethren, with the late Grand Officers, attending in a regular procession, they were carried to the Stone Chapel; where an animated eulogium was delivered by Brother Perez Morton at their request . . .

It was Paul Revere who identified the body as Warren's, by two artificial teeth which he had wired into his friend's mouth shortly before the Battle of Lexington. In addition to his work as a goldsmith and engraver, Paul Revere practiced dentistry from 1768 until the time of the Revolution. As a Lodge officer, Revere was also in the masonic procession during Warren's funeral, and afterwards was one of three masons selected to thank Brother Morton for his address and request a copy for the press.[60]

Despite the display of masonic fraternity during Joseph Warren's funeral, the masons did not meet throughout 1776. It was not until December 1776 that the brethren "who had been dispersed during the war" were "now generally collected." In February 1777, a summons was issued for a meeting to settle the question of electing a new Grand Master. The summons was sent "to all Masters and Wardens under this Jurisdiction to Assemble here on the 7th March in Order to Consult upon + elect a Grand Master for this State." The summons resulted in a meeting on March 8, 1777, when the Grand Lodge

together with the Delegates of the other Lodges under this jurisdiction, taking into consideration the absolute necessity of having a Grand Master of our own appointment for this State, Have thought fit to Constitute, appoint . . . and Elect our trusty and well beloved Brother Joseph Webb, Esqr . . .

Webb was elected Grand Master to serve until "Friday June Next," while Paul Revere was chosen Junior Grand Warden, a step up from the position of Deacon that he had held from 1769 to 1774.[61]

The election of a new Grand Master in 1777 was an act of masonic self-preservation. After the untimely death of Joseph Warren

How to assemble the Grand Lodge, with regularity, was . . . a serious question, as the commission of the Grand Master had died with him, + the deputy had no power independent of his nomination + appointment.

Consequently, "experiencing the necessity of preserving an intercourse of the brethren, + the want of a proper establishment, to soften the rigours of an active + distressing war . . ." the masons, on March 8, 1777, "proceeded to the formation of an independent Grand

Lodge . . ." Although the masons acted independent of Scotland in electing Webb, it was the only way to keep the Lodge functioning until the military situation was resolved.[62]

Despite military obligations, Paul Revere continued to hold masonic offices throughout the late 1770s, although his participation was not as constant as it had been before the War years. He served as Master of St. Andrew's Lodge for two years from 1778 to 1779 and as Junior Grand Warden in the Massachusetts Grand Lodge from 1777 to 1779. By April 10, 1776, soon after the British evacuation of Boston, Paul Revere was commissioned as a major in the regiment raised for Boston's defense. By fall, he was a lieutenant colonel commanding the garrison at Castle Island in Boston harbor. His superior was Colonel Thomas Crafts, a fellow mason with whom Revere served on many masonic committees, once even requesting "his Regt Musick" for a feast day celebration. Paul Revere's duties on Castle Island diverted his attention from masonic affairs. Although a Grand Lodge officer, he attended only half of the meetings held by that Lodge between 1777 and 1779. In St. Andrew's Lodge, where he held no office through 1776-1777, he attended fewer meetings. Of the forty-eight meetings held by St. Andrew's Lodge in 1777, he attended only fifteen, but he was present at the annual election of officers on December 2, 1777, where he was chosen as Master for the coming year. Possibly due to his frequent absences from Lodge meetings at this time, Paul Revere was not the first choice of the assembled brethren for Master, but the third. The first two candidates declined to serve. Throughout his masonic career, Paul Revere never refused an office, and, ever true to his responsibilities, his Lodge attendance increased dramatically when he had an office to fulfill. Although Revere was still stationed on Castle Island when he was elected Master of St. Andrew's Lodge in 1778 and 1779, he attended most of the meetings and Lodge activities continued as usual.[63]

Although little reference is made to the celebration of feast days while Paul Revere was Master, there was a lively interest in St. Andrew's Lodge, which continuously admitted new members and conferred degrees. Charitable activities also continued. Along with the charity towards "strange brethren" and prisoners of war, Revere himself pleaded to his fellow masons for Moses Deshon, a Past Master whose "circumstances were such as realy deserved their notices." £32.6 were collected for his relief. The Lodge raised its fees during the two years, bought tickets in both the United States and Massachusetts State Lotteries, and received monetary gifts totaling $170. The Lodge also received gifts of two chairs and "a number of elegant Brass Sconces." In evidence of the growing number of masons in their ranks, the Lodge also purchased three dozen aprons in December 1778. Not every individual desiring entrance into St. Andrew's Lodge was accepted. In December 1778, "Brother Pulsifer proposed Mr. Manasseh Marston," but on January 15, 1779, "Mr. Marston hav stood the usual time was balloted for and had three negatives." Manasseh Marston and Paul Revere were neighbors, the rear of Revere's North Square property bordering on Marston's. Although he was denied admittance at this time, Manasseh Marston became a member of St. Andrew's Lodge on December 12, 1781.[64]

While still Master of St. Andrew's Lodge, military duty called Paul Revere away from Boston in June 1779. In late June, he was ordered to accompany an expedition to Castine, Maine in Penobscot Bay, where the British had recently erected a fortification. By July 25, Revere and the forces had arrived in Penobscot Bay. The expedition was a dismal failure, lasting only until August 13. Less than a week later, Paul Revere was again back in Boston commanding on Castle Island. On September 6, 1779, he was suddenly asked to resign his position due to charges of misconduct resulting from the Penobscot campaign. Revere stoutly denied the charges and repeatedly demanded a court martial to clear his name. The affair was not settled until he was granted his court martial in 1782, at which time the charges were dismissed. Probably due to the Penobscot affair and its unfortunate aftermath, Revere was not present at the meetings of St. Andrew's Lodge from August through November 1779. On November 30, 1779, when new officers were elected for 1780, it was voted that "the thanks of this Lodge be given to Paul Revere, Esq. as Master of this Lodge for his service these 2 years past. . ." In the Grand Lodge, "Bro. Col. Revere" also did not attend any meetings from June to December 1779. Revere's attendance at St. Andrew's Masters' Lodge was minimal during the late 1770s.[65]

Although Paul Revere's masonic participation had been interrupted by military duty, the disruption was only temporary. In late 1779, he resumed his masonic activity and served on several committees in St. Andrew's Lodge during 1780. In November, 1779, Revere was one of a standing committee of seven concerning "the Rent agreeable to the appreciation or Depreciation of the Currency," referring to the Green Dragon Tavern. On March 9, 1780, although Revere was not even present, he was appointed to a committee with four other high ranking masons. In May, he was one of five masons directed to "Revise the Bylaws." By November of 1780, Revere was again elected Master of St. Andrew's Lodge, a position he held through 1781 and 1782. During this time he attended meetings faithfully, proposed new members and served on every major committee raised while he was Master. Lodge meetings were lively and well attended, with usually twenty or more members present and at least five to ten visitors. Degrees were conferred at every meeting and, with several exceptions, meetings were regularly held. It was noted in the Lodge minutes of November 30, 1781 that the Lodge would not be meeting as usual on the second Thursday of December because that day was "appointed a Day of Thanksgiving by Authority."[66]

While serving as Lodge Master, Paul Revere not only directed, but actively participated in Lodge business. He even personally dispensed charity, a task usually performed by the Secretary or Treasurer. On December 14, 1780, the hat went around for Alex Burnett and "there was gathered 532 dollars and Delivered him by Ye Master." Another petitioner, on March 8, 1781, was awarded $422 which was "gathered and delivered him by the R. W. Master." Paul Revere also served on committees. In February, 1782, a committee of nine, including Revere and other officers, was raised to petition the Grand Lodge for a charter securing St. Andrew's "rank of Precedency." Having been chartered November 30, 1756, St. Andrew's held rank as the oldest Lodge under the jurisdiction of the Massachusetts Grand Lodge. For some reason never explained, almost nine months later it was moved that "the vote passed the 25th February last be reconsidered respecting the petition to the Grand Lodge for a charter." Revere also served on a committee of seven in March 1782 to petition the Commonwealth of Massachusetts to incorporate under the name of St. Andrew's Lodge.[67]

During Revere's term as Master of St. Andrew's Lodge, the Lodge also considered selling the Green Dragon Tavern. In March 1781, Paul Revere served on a committee of seven appointed to investigate "the practicality of disposing of Masons' Hall and purchasing some Convenient spot of land and building a new Lodge Room . . ." This committee must have done little between March and May because, on May 10, Revere was made the Chairman and Brother Joseph Webb was fined for neglect "agreeable to the By-Laws." By May 18, Revere and the committee reported "that there is a spot near the Common for sale which they think will answer for the above purpose." After considering the matter, the Lodge resolved "that the above affair should subside for y' present." The Lodge continued to meet in the Green Dragon Tavern and no further mention was ever made of selling the property while Paul Revere was active in St. Andrew's Lodge. It is never stated why the masons wished to abandon Masons' Hall, but the property was probably in need of repair. Only two years later, in 1783, when the property was inspected, the following repairs were ordered: "Privy House to be repaired, top of the mansion house, a new pump in the Cellar, Stairs to be mended, Front Room and Kitchen floor to make new, a new penthouse and a window shutter to be made." Meanwhile, the Hall continued in use by St. Andrew's Lodge and others. In December 1782, as Paul Revere's term as Master was ending, he postponed the choice of officers from Monday to Thursday so that the Massachusetts Charitable Society could use the Hall. This year as Master was the last that Paul Revere would ever serve with St. Andrew's, as momentous events beginning in December 1782 eventually drove him away from his chosen Lodge.[68]

VI

INDEPENDENCE AND TURMOIL

Despite the death of Joseph Warren and the military tenor of the times, Grand Lodge affairs continued relatively undisturbed throughout the later war years. Joseph Webb was elected Grand Master for every year from 1777 to 1782, and Paul Revere served in the offices of Junior and Senior Grand Warden throughout this period. It was not until 1782 that the Massachusetts Grand Lodge took a bold step which would alter Paul Revere's future as a mason. On June 10, 1782, the Grand Lodge voted "that a Committee be Appointed to Draught Resolutions explanatory of the Powers and Authority of this Grand Lodge respecting the Extent and Meaning of its Jurisdiction . . ." Paul Revere, who was at this time Senior Grand Warden, was on this committee, which delivered its report to the Grand Lodge on December 6, 1782.[69]

The report, which was to have a significant impact on Massachusetts Freemasonry, examined the conduct of the Grand Lodge and defended the independent election of Joseph Webb in 1777. In the report, Paul Revere and his brethren explained

> That the Commission from the Grand Lodge of Scotland granted to our late Grand Master Joseph Warren Esqr having died with him and of Course his Deputy whose Appointment was derived from his Nomination being no longer in existance, they saw themselves, without a Head, & without a Single Grand Officer, and of Course it was evident that not Only the Grand Lodge, but all the particular Lodges under its Jurisdiction must Cease to Assemble, the Brethren be dispersed, the Pennyless go unassisted, the Craft Languish + Ancient masonry be extinct in this Part [of the] World.

As the 1782 report continued, it justified the decision, made in 1777, to reconvene and elect a new Grand Master in order to "preserve the Intercourse of the Brethren." The masons recognized

> That the Political Head of this Country having destroyed All connection + Correspondence between the Subjects of these States + the Country from which the Grand Lodge originally derived its Commis-

sioned Authority, and the Principles of the Craft inculcating on its professors Submission to the Commands of the Civil Authority of the Country they Reside in, the Brethren did Assume an Elective Supremacy, + under it Chose a Grand Master + Grand Officers, and Erected a Grand Lodge with Independent Powers & Perogatives, to be exercised however, on Principles consistant with, + Subordinate to the Regulations pointed out in the Constitution of Ancient Masonry.

The committee concluded that the actions of the Grand Lodge in 1777 were "dictated by Principles of the Clearest Necessity, founded in the Highest Reason and Warranted by Precedents of the Most approved Authority."[70]

The 1782 report, which was signed by Paul Revere and three other masons, concluded with a series of resolutions, which the committee strongly urged that the Grand Lodge adopt. The resolutions included the following bold declaration.

That this Grand Lodge be forever hereafter known + Called by the Name of the Massachusetts Grand Lodge of Ancient Masons, and, that it is free and Independent in its Government + Official Authority of any other Grand Lodge, or Grand Master in the Universe.

After going through the report "paragraph by paragraph," the Grand Lodge accepted the document, including the above controversial resolution. For all Ancient Masons, the resolution of the Grand Lodge posed a serious question of allegiance. By declaring itself "free and independent," the Massachusetts Grand Lodge was officially breaking its connection to the parent Grand Lodge in Scotland. St. Andrew's Lodge would also be forced to decide whether its loyalty remained with Scotland, or with the newly independent Massachusetts Grand Lodge. For Paul Revere, who had a hand in writing the resolution of independence, but who also had strong ties to both Lodges, the decision must have been a difficult one.[71]

St. Andrew's Lodge immediately responded by calling a Lodge of Emergency on December 16, 1782, at which the members took a vote whether to acknowledge the independent Grand Lodge. Of forty-nine members present, a majority of thirty voted "Nay." A committee was assigned to draft a letter to the Grand Lodge informing its members of the negative vote. The Grand Lodge received the letter by December 24, 1782 when, at a Special Meeting, a committee of five was raised to meet with St. Andrew's Lodge "upon the Subject of their Letter on Refusing to Acknowledge the Independency of this Grand Lodge." The Grand Lodge also felt the need to explain its independency to the Scottish Grand Master, whom it wrote in January 1783, presenting "the Reasons why the Grand Lodge in Commonwealth [of] Massachusetts Assumed to Themselves that Dignity." The Grand

Lodge also sent a circular letter to all the Lodges under its jurisdiction "on the subject of Independence of this Grand Lodge." St. Andrew's Lodge still disapproved, stating that the declaration of independence was "inconsistent with the principles of Masonry necessary to be observed for the good of the craft." Despite its disapproval, St. Andrew's decided to pay dues and send representatives to the Massachusetts Grand Lodge "until there is a peace between this state and Scotland, at which Time this Lodge will determine whether they will be under Scotland or America." It would wait until the war was over.[72]

With the final treaty signed on September 3, 1783, the American War for Independence was officially won and over. Two months later, St. Andrew's Lodge again raised the question of its allegiance to the Grand Lodge of Scotland. On January 22, 1784, fifty-two masons met in the Long Room where they voted "that all those who are in favor of continuing under the Grand Lodge of Scotland retire to the North side of the Lodge, and those who acknowledge the authority of the Massachusetts Grand Lodge would retire to the South Side." The Wardens counted heads and found the majority again with Scotland (See Appendix 3.) For Paul Revere, a vote for Scotland would have meant denouncing the Grand Lodge in which he had just been personally chosen by Grand Master John Warren, brother of the late Joseph Warren, to serve as Deputy Grand Master, a position which had evolved "for the better and easier and more honourable discharge" of the Grand Master's office. Revere walked to the South side of the Lodge, throwing his vote with John Warren, the Massachusetts Grand Lodge and the new Republic he had helped create and defend.[73]

Repercussions swiftly followed. Two weeks later, St. Andrew's voted that "no person shall be admitted a member of this Lodge who acknowledge the authority of the Assumed Massachusetts Grand Lodge." Revere suddenly found himself ousted from the Lodge which he had served as Master only two years earlier, but he was not alone. Twenty-two fellow masons had voted as he did, while only slightly over thirty had voted to remain with Scotland. The membership of St. Andrew's Lodge was reduced by nearly one-half. On February 5, 1784, the minority was given an opportunity to repent.

> If they or either of them shall appear at Masons Hall on the next monthly Lodge and there explicitly acknowledge the sole supremacy and exclusive jurisdiction of the Grand Lodge of Scotland over St. Andrews Lodge . . . and shall disavow all the doings, authority and jurisdiction of every kind of such persons as composes the body *assuming* to themselves the name of Massachusetts Grand Lodge-then such as shall so acknowledge the Grand Lodge of Scotland as above mentioned shall again be considered as members of St. Andrews Lodge.

Paul Revere did come to St. Andrew's Lodge at the next meeting, but not to change his vote.[74]

On February 12, 1784, Paul Revere and four fellow masons arrived at St. Andrew's Lodge. The Tyler stopped them at the door and informed the brethren inside that "a number of persons who wanted to speak with the Lodge were in waiting." The Tyler was told that "St. Andrews Lodge knew of no committee that they had employed upon any business this evening" whereas, after some debate, Revere and his companions "came in the Lodge and said they were a committee from a number of agrieved brethren who looked upon themselves as members of this Lodge . . ." Revere, clearly the leader of the group, was told that they would have to make their proposals in writing "which would be candidly attended to." It was recorded that "the Brethren who state themselves *the agrieved* do not choose to make any propositions to St. Andrews Lodge-in writing." With this reception, Revere's committee must have left the Lodge. If any further communications took place at this meeting, the minutes did not record it.[75]

The reply in writing came one month later in March 1784. It was signed by Paul Revere, his four companions of the previous month and two additional masons, one being Robert Hichborn. Although the content of the letter was not recorded, its impact was clear. On March 25, 1784, a special meeting of St. Andrew's Lodge was held because of it. The minutes record that "Mr. Sam¹ Barrett the Treasurer of this Lodge has been sued by Paul Revere, Esq. and Mr. Nath Fellows for the sum of £48," the lawsuit resulting from "a supposed right which they have to part of the stock of this Lodge." Paul Revere and his "agrieved Brethren" did not view their actions as wrong. Being half of St. Andrew's Lodge, they felt justly entitled to half of the Lodge funds, with which they intended to continue meeting under a commission from the Massachusetts Grand Lodge. The lawsuit was probably a course of last resort, since nine days earlier, on March 16, 1784, mention is made that "Paul Revere and others offer to divide the property of St. Andrew's according to numbers." Seemingly, the offer was denied. St. Andrew's had already sent a letter to the Massachusetts Grand Lodge on March 4, informing that Lodge of its intention to "retain their ancient charter from Scotland and to consider themselves no longer subject to the control of this Grand Lodge . . ." The Grand Lodge recognized their intentions and declared that "all Connection and Debates, between this Grand Lodge, and the Lodge of St. Andrew are at an End." For Paul Revere and his minority, it was too late for compromise.[76]

From the viewpoint of St. Andrew's Lodge, the behavior of the minority was scandalous. Not only did they lose all rights of membership through their "unworthy conduct," but they revealed "minds devoid of the true spirits of Masonry and greedily desirous of that property which by our Charter we are bound to preserve for the support of decay'd brethren, widows and orphans." The necessity of legal action disturbed the St. Andrew's masons, but they resolved to "oppose by all lawful means the demands of said Revere and Fellows and of any others who may have found rights on such imaginery suppositions . . ." The masons of St. Andrew's Lodge were concerned that "the conduct of our late Brethren will if publically scanned devolve the highest dishonor on the Crafts; and give a . . . fatal stab to the reputation of masonry . . ." Differences were usually kept within the Lodge, but Revere had made it a public affair through the lawsuit. St. Andrew's Lodge protested and declared

> to all masonic brethren in particular and to the World at Large that it has ever been our constant and invariable desire to have had the fictitious grievances of the said Revere and Fellows discussed and decided by a few candid Brethren mutually chosen by them and this Lodge . . .

The affair was finally settled in this manner. Although in March 1784, it appeared that the case would go to court, by October the lawsuit had been settled privately. In a letter from St. Andrew's Lodge to the Scottish Grand Lodge on October 7, 1784, mention is made that the lawsuit "has since been settled by a reference of five brother masons who gave them [Revere] a certain proportion of the whole stock belonging to St. Andrews Lodge, in consequence of which we are considerably reduced as to our funds."[77]

VII

ENTER RISING STATES LODGE

Due to the difficulties with St. Andrew's Lodge in early 1784, Paul Revere and his minority formed a new Lodge, also named "St. Andrew's," which received a charter from the Massachusetts Grand Lodge. Paul Revere served as Treasurer, with Nathaniel Fellows as Master. One of the first meetings was held at the Bunch of Grapes Tavern on State Street on March 29, 1784. By this time, a code of bylaws had already been established "and the whole unanimously aggreed to." The Lodge also voted to hold future meetings at the Royal Exchange Tavern until further notice. The brethren procured many Lodge necessities during March of 1784. (See Illustration 4.) The first entry in Revere's account book is for "Silver Jewels for Mar, Ward^n, Trea, Sec^y, Dea^n, 2 Steward + Tyler" at a cost of £13.10. For the "materials + making Colars for hanging jewels" the expense was £5.13. The Lodge also purchased six Ladles, "3p of Candlesticks" and "3p Snuffers." For storage, the Lodge procured a small trunk, a "Lock and hinges for chest" and a lock for the closet, possibly for the use of the Stewards. The Lodge also paid "M^r. Greens Bill for Books" as well as purchasing "paper for Sec^y," a "marble Cov^d Book," a pewter ink chest, and cloth and nails for a desk. Also in March, Revere paid £4.10 for "Engraving Copper Plate for Summons" and £1.12 for printing 400 impressions of the same.[78]

For the first year of its existence, the new St. Andrew's Lodge held most of its meetings at the Royal Exchange Tavern. For every meeting held there, Revere paid "Mrs. Gray for room" usually £1. For meetings held at "Col. Marston's State Street," better known as the Bunch of Grapes Tavern, Revere records payment of "Br. Marston's Bill," which was seldom lower than £3.6. Revere paid these bills on or before the meeting date of the Lodge. The Tyler and Secretary were also paid for their services. These bills, including dues paid to the Massachusetts Grand Lodge, account for most of the regular expenses of the Lodge paid by Revere as Treasurer. On the opposite side of the ledger, Revere received cash from "making," "members," "visitors" and quarterly dues. A fee was paid whenever anyone was made a mason, as well as when visitors attended the Lodge meetings. During 1784, there were regularly two to seven visitors present at every meeting, in addition to fourteen to twenty regular Lodge members. Candidates were proposed and made masons or members at every meeting. However, by July 1784, it was clear to Revere that the Lodge income was not sufficient to defray expenses. He motioned that a "committee be chosen to inquire into the Lodge Debts and Propose a method to Defray them and point out what may be best to be done with the Government Securities . . ." The committee made its report on September 27, 1784, with Revere as spokesman. He reported that

> this Lodge owes about Sixty-five Pounds, that the Present Stock of the Lodge is in Government Securities and that were they now Sold they would not fetch more than what the Lodge Owes: That the Interest due on Said Securities is nearly as much as they will fetch: That if the Members who have advanced nothing for the Lodge will each of them advance two years Quartridge they will be able to pay the Debts and save their Securities.

By 1786, when Revere recorded his final "Ballance for New Treasurer," the Lodge was no longer in debt, according to his accounts.[79]

Paul Revere served as Treasurer of the new Lodge from 1784 until 1786. On May 31, 1784, it was voted that "as this Lodge has so lately made Choice of Officers, Twas' mov'd and seconded that the same Officers should be ballotted for and they were Unanimously Chosen for the Ensuing Year." Along with his financial responsibility as Treasurer, Revere contributed often to Lodge committees. On October 25, 1784, two committees were raised, both of which included Revere. The first was appointed "to find a Place for This Lodge to meet the Next Lodge Night." The second committee was chosen "to furnish a Copper Plate for the Use of Summoning the Lodge Together." Since Revere made officers' jewels and copper plate engravings for other Lodges (see Appendix 5), it is possible that he also made these for his own Lodge, since he did make a seal for the Lodge in 1784. (See Illustration 5.) In February 1785, it was voted to remove the Lodge to Brother Stodder's. Revere was one of a committee raised "to aggree with Br. Stodder for the uses of the Room." Repeated payments to "Br. Stodder Bill" after April 1785 indicate that this is where the Lodge was meeting. In the absence of Master Fellows, Jonathan Stodder often served as Lodge Master. He did so on October 25, 1784, when it was noted that "Br. Revere, by the Desire of the Master took the Chair and gave Lecture." By February 28, 1785, Paul Revere himself was listed as Master, while a letter of resignation was read and accepted from Worshipful Brother Fellows. In March 1785, several Lodges asked the Grand Lodge for permission to hold a convention "to consider the present State of Masonry in this commonwealth . . ." Paul Revere, Jonathan Stodder and Norton Brailsford, all officers, attended the convention as representatives of their new Lodge, at a cost to the

Lodge of £1.8.6. The meeting was a successful one. It was held at Warren Hall in Charlestown, where "a candid discussion served to strengthen and cement the authority of the Grand Lodge, and the result was *harmony beneficience* and *good will*."[80]

Although no longer an officer in the Massachusetts Grand Lodge by 1785, Paul Revere regularly attended the meetings and paid dues as a representative of his new Lodge. Originally called by the name of "St. Andrew's ," Revere's Lodge received a new name by late 1784. In July 1784, when Revere proposed that a committee be raised to examine the Lodge debts, the committee was also instructed to "propose another name for this Lodge." By August 30, the name of Rising States Lodge was suggested. A committee was raised to petition the Grand Lodge concerning the name change, which committee delivered the petition by September 2, 1784. On that date, the Grand Lodge noted that "a Petition of St. Andrew's Lodge N°1 holding under this Jurisdiction" was received, requesting "a renewal of their Charter with the alteration of the name to 'Rising States'." By the meeting of October 25, 1784, the Lodge was referred to by its new name. The masons probably changed the name only on account of the confusion created by having two Lodges of St. Andrew in Boston. As the first Ancient Lodge in America, founded November 30, 1756, the original St. Andrew's Lodge had held the prestigious rank of being the oldest Lodge in the jurisdiction. Now that St. Andrew's had denied its affiliation with the Massachusetts Grand Lodge, the masons of Rising States Lodge wished to take its place and "hold rank as the oldest Lodge under the jurisdiction," using the 1756 founding date of St. Andrew's Lodge as its own. Most of the members of Rising States Lodge, such as Paul Revere, had been long-standing, devoted members of St. Andrew's Lodge for many years and desired to obtain a new charter "holding the former Precedence." In 1789, Rising States Lodge again applied to the Grand Lodge for a new Charter, after which the Grand Lodge voted that "a new Charter be granted to the Rising States Lodge, they paying the Customary fees and that they have Rank as they stand upon the books." This question of rank was due to be a source of trouble for Rising States Lodge in the future.[81]

Paul Revere was a regular officeholder in Rising States Lodge from its founding. He served as Treasurer from March 1784 until April 1786. At several meetings, he was listed both as Treasurer and Deputy Grand Master (D:G:M), referring to Revere's office in the Massachusetts Grand Lodge. When Nathaniel Fellows resigned as Master on February 28, 1785, Revere served in the position while still acting as Treasurer. He also represented the Lodge as Master at a joint meeting of the Lodges held at the Bunch of Grapes Tavern in March 1785. At the election of June 1785, Revere was again chosen as Treasurer until 1786. In 1787, Revere was elected Master of the Lodge, being re-elected in 1788. Paul Revere, Jr. served under his father as a Steward these two years. Five years earlier, at the meeting of December 27, 1784, Amos Lincoln had proposed Paul Revere, Jr. to be made a mason in the Lodge. At the next meeting, he was "voted unanimously and was accordingly made." Amos Lincoln was a son-in-law of Paul Revere. He regularly attended meetings and served as a Lodge officer by 1785. Paul Revere was still Master of Rising States Lodge in March 1789, and was again selected in 1791, with Amos Lincoln as Senior Warden and Paul Revere, Jr. as Secretary. At the election of December 1792, Revere was again chosen as Master to serve through 1793. (See Appendix 2.)[82]

Like every other Lodge in the jurisdiction, Rising States Lodge was chartered by the Grand Lodge of Massachusetts and was subject to its inspection and control. Such an inspection occurred on March 30, 1789 when the annual visitation of the Grand Lodge took place. At that time, Paul Revere was serving as Master of Rising States Lodge and Moses M. Hays was Grand Master. According to the Grand Lodge, it was "the duty of the G:Master + his Wardens annually to visit and Inspect the Lodges under this jurisdiction, either by themselves or their Proxies." When the Grand Lodge officers arrived at Rising States Lodge, it was recorded that "we now do ourselves the Honor of such (a) Visit, + Crave the favor of Perusing your books & Records." As Master of Rising States Lodge, Paul Revere then "Gave a lecture, which did them infinite Honor, and met the approbation of the Grand Lodge." The visit was satisfactory for everyone concerned, and Paul Revere acknowledged its success by delivering a brief address. In the name of his Lodge, Revere offered

> thanks for the favor of this visit, and for this mark of Love + Affection of the Grand Lodge—It was a great addition to the pleasure of the Lodge, to find the Grand Master so much gratified, in viewing the Harmony + Decorum of the Lodge, And they presume to flatter themselves, that by a steady Perseverance of such Cultivation, and travelling in pursuit of Virtue and Morality, and being Circumspect As to the persons we admit into our Society; We shall continue to merit the Approbation of the Grand Lodge.

Revere then stated that a list of officers, members and initiates during the past year would be given to the Massachusetts Grand Lodge.[83]

VIII

THE MASSACHUSETTS GRAND LODGE—POST WAR DECADE

During the decade after its declaration of independence in 1782, the Massachusetts Grand Lodge grew and struggled along with the new nation. Although masonic duties continued as usual, the Grand Lodge maintained an uneasy existence, constantly fighting to assert and enforce its authority. Paul Revere served as a Lodge officer for several years during this decade, and he attended meetings with characteristic regularity. Revere often contributed to Lodge committees, which were raised at nearly every meeting to discuss every type of Lodge business. He served on several committees appointed to examine Lodge accounts, a task usually performed around the time that officers were chosen. In June 1785, he and two others were directed to "examine the State of the G^d Lodge Accounts" while in 1787, 1789 and 1790, he worked with the committees that settled the Treasurer's accounts.[84]

Through committee work, Paul Revere also dealt regularly with those rules and documents that kept the Lodge running smoothly. In September 1783, Revere was included on a committee of seven created "for the Purpose of Forming Rules & Regulations for the Government of the Grand Lodge." At the next meeting in October, the Lodge voted that the rules and regulations "after being read Paragraph by Paragraph be Accepted." At the same meeting, a Committee, which included Revere, was formed to see that one hundred copies of the regulations were printed, which would then be distributed to every member. Several references to printing a book of Constitutions also included Revere. In 1786, it was mentioned that "a Committee be appointed to draft a book of Constitutions for the Massachusetts Grand Lodge." Paul Revere seconded the motion and was also included on the committee. Progress on the book of Constitutions must have been slow, since two years later, a committee was appointed

> to procure the printing of a book of Constitutions—provided it shall not be attended with Expense to the Grand Lodge; if however this

cannot be Effected; then the present Regulations are to be printed for the Benefit of the Lodges under the jurisdiction . . .

Paul Revere was also chosen for this committee.[85]

The primary purpose of a Grand Lodge is to charter Lodges and monitor the behavior of Lodges and individuals, and it was these activities which consumed much of the Grand Lodge's time. As a senior officer, Paul Revere assisted in performing these tasks, particularly the chartering of new Lodges. Numerous Lodges were chartered during the 1780s, not all of which were in Massachusetts. In 1781, the Grand Lodge received a petition requesting a charter for a Lodge in Litchfield, Connecticut, which it decided to grant "In as much as no Grand Lodge, nor Grand Master, Ever has, nor does at Present Exist in Said State." Following this example, the Grand Lodge also issued a charter for a Lodge in Vermont only five months later "on the Same Conditions that Charters have heretofore been Granted by this Grand Lodge to Petitioners from States of New Hampshire and Connecticutt." In the same way, the Grand Lodge also issued a charter for North Star Lodge in Vermont, as well as for a Lodge in Keene, New Hampshire. In 1788, Paul Revere was one of several masons who investigated a petition for a Lodge in Hanover, New Hampshire. It was voted that the charter be granted.[86]

Once chartered, Lodges were periodically visited and problems investigated. Visitations served to insure the proper functioning of the Lodges as well as reinforcing the authority of the Grand Lodge. Although local visits were most convenient, such as that to Rising States Lodge in 1789, the Grand Lodge also traveled to more distant Lodges. On June 10 and 11, 1793, the Grand Lodge visited Trinity Lodge at Lancaster and Morning Star Lodge at Worcester, examining records and installing officers. Paul Revere was present on both occasions. Revere also participated frequently on the many committees formed to handle Lodge problems. When the charters of both Essex and Amity Lodges were returned to the Grand Lodge, it was Paul Revere who presented the documents and was "possessed of the particulars." It is not mentioned why the charters were returned. It was also the duty of the Grand Lodge to see that Lodges were properly constituted. In 1786, Revere and several others served on a committee to investigate "a Lodge at Danbury by the Name of Union, + also of another at Salisbury by the name of Montgomery whose time of Creation + Record of Charter is not to be found in the G. Lodge Books." Problems with Lodges often involved money. Such was the case with Wooster Lodge, which had been chartered in Colchester, Connecticut in 1781. By 1789, a Grand Lodge committee was formed, including Revere, "to call on Bro: Brailsford in ten days for the Ballance due from Wooster Lodge."[87]

Numerous cases of improper conduct were also brought to the

Lodge's attention in the 1780s, several dealing with Friendship Lodge, a French Lodge which had been constituted in Boston in January 1780, later rechartered under the name of Perfect Union Lodge. By September 1780, George DeFrance, an officer of Friendship Lodge, had been accused of "malconduct" and he requested that the Grand Lodge investigate the charges. In January 1781, several members of the same Lodge issued charges against their late Master Duplassius, while in September of the same year, Master Jeatau submitted a complaint against the late Treasurer, Brother Jareau. Paul Revere was on the committee directed to contact Jareau and "know what he has to offer in Vindication of the Late Conduct Charged against him." By March 1790, nine years later, charges of "Conduct highly unbecoming a Mason" were also directed against John Jutau, possibly the same "Master Jeatau" of Friendship Lodge mentioned above, who was then serving as Senior Grand Warden of the Massachusetts Grand Lodge. The Lodge considered it a duty "not only to investigate the Misconduct of its officers, and to Censure the Guilty, but also in Case of false Accusation to Vindicate the Innocent, and to discountenance the Accuser." Unfortunately, the accusations proved true and the Grand Lodge concluded, among other things, that "his (Bro:J) having two wives at one and the same time is fully Established." Declaring that Jutau's conduct was "highly derogatory to the laws of Morality, Society and Honor, and diametrically Opposed to the Principles of Masonry," the Lodge voted to remove Jutau from his Grand Lodge office and erase his name from the books.[88]

While charges and accusations were usually presented to the Grand Lodge for investigation, Lodges would occasionally conduct their own inquiries into improper conduct and inform the Grand Lodge afterwards for its approval. Such was the case of Daniel Bayley, who earned the displeasure of St. Peter's Lodge in 1781. After "Examination + Just Tryal," that Lodge found him "Guilty of Mutiny, Blasphemy, Conniving at Theft and Misrepresentation of their Lodge to the Grand Lodge, for which Crimes, as Masons the Body Finally Exclude him for EVER." The Grand Lodge approved of the proceedings. The case of George DeFrance of Friendship Lodge ended differently. Despite the charges, the Grand Lodge ruled that DeFrance should again "be held in Equal Estimation, Friendship + Brotherly Love." This decision, which was recorded September 1781, was fortunate for Paul Revere, and perhaps Revere played a part in it, as he had been renting his North Square home to a man named George DeFrance since May of 1780.[89]

While problems with the conduct of masons and the legality of Lodges were not unusual, cases such as those of Daniel Bayley and Jutau are exceptional in their infrequency. They are almost the only two misconduct cases which appear in the Grand Lodge minutes from 1782 to 1792. What seemed to trouble the Grand Lodge more during this period was a persistent trend of neglect on the part of its constituent Lodges in sending dues and representatives to the quarterly meetings of the Grand Lodge. The problem resurfaced with irritating regularity and, as a firm believer in the obedience of Lodges, Paul Revere was involved with many of the committees that were appointed to compel the Lodges' cooperation. As early as January 1781, the Grand Lodge voted to write to the Lodges which "have Neglected a Representation," warning them that "if they Continue such Neglect, a Forfiture of their Charters will be the Consiquence." Five months later the issue was raised again and Paul Revere was one of the three masons selected to "write to the deficient Lodges in very Plain Terms." With the resolution of independence in December 1782, the question of Lodge representation was superceded by other concerns, and even after two years, the Grand Lodge was still working to define its authority. In December 1784, a committee was formed to "prepare a plan . . . by which the jurisdiction of said Grand Lodge may be positively ascertained." Paul Revere was on this committee, which was also directed to "take into Consideration the delinquency of Several Lodges holding Charters under this jurisdiction."[90]

After this point, the problem of delinquent Lodges was raised every year, for which the Grand Lodge never seemed to find a satisfactory solution. In December 1785, the Grand Lodge motioned to "immediately summon all the Lodges to a prompt Representation, + due Payment of their Quarterages + Arrearages due." In September 1786, the Grand Lodge threatened to dissolve Lodges which failed to pay dues and send representatives or proxies. By 1787, Paul Revere was on a committee "chosen to assist the G:S: in Collecting the Dues + devising means to obtain a better Representation in Grand Lodge." By March 1788, the Grand Lodge was out of patience. A committee was created, which included Revere, to

> consider the present State of the G^d Lodge . . . to report to the Grand Master such Lodges as in their Opinion have been delinquent, That the Grand Master be Requested to inform the Officers of such Lodges, that unless they are represented at the next Quarterly Communication in June, and Sufficient Reasons are given, Why their Dues have not been paid, and why they have not been Represented, their Lodges will be Erased from the Grand Lodge Books, and they no longer Considered as Regular Societies of Free + Accepted Masons, under this Jurisdiction.[91]

True to their word, the Grand Lodge must have expelled Lodges at the June meeting because reference is made, in September 1788, to Lodges which were "lately struck out of the G:L: Books." Paul Revere was appointed to two committees at the September meeting, both of which dealt with the delinquent Lodges. Since the expelled Lodges were required to return their charters to the Grand Lodge, one committee was directed to write to the Lodges requesting the return of their charters by the next meeting, while the other was raised to "adjust, commute + finally Settle Accounts." Two years later, by 1790, the problem of delinquent Lodges had not improved, and the Grand Lodge was compelled to admit that "a General Inattention to the Grand Lodge, and a want of strict adherence to its Laws + Regulations, has tended to lessen its importance." The Grand Lodge did not even have enough money to pay its debts. It concluded that "every Lodge not represented and neglecting to pay for the space of twelve months shall positively forfeit their connection with the Grand Lodge."[92]

While the persistence of delinquent Lodges can be interpreted as an indication of deeper trouble, the problem itself was not a new one and it was certainly not limited to the decade of 1782–1792. It was clearly more pronounced during this period, which could reflect the economic hardship of the post-war depression, rather than a general lack of interest in masonic activities. A related trend was the curious absence throughout the mid-1780s of the June and December celebrations of the feasts of St. John, when the Grand Lodge repeatedly voted not to hold the festivals. Since the Grand Lodge was dependent for its support upon the constituent Lodges, many of which were neglecting to pay dues, perhaps the festivals were not being held for lack of funds. The December feast in 1780 was held as usual, with Paul Revere helping "to Conduct the Business of said Feast." The Grand Lodge had also planned to celebrate the Feast of St. John in December 1781, but reversed its decision "on the Principle that the . . . Prices are beyond the ability of many Brethren to Support, without Apparent Injury to their Families." By the following June, it was voted to hold the feast and Paul Revere was involved with the committees created to rent Faneuil Hall and find some suitable person to deliver the sermon. In June 1783, the Feast was also held with a "Procession, Oration + Charge" and Revere again took part in arranging for the oration and the dinners. By December 1783, the Lodge voted not to have "any Public Procession or Entertainment in the present Inclement Season" but encouraged the constituent Lodges to "Celebrate the Feast in Form at their own Particular Lodge Rooms." No explanation is offered for the lack of celebrations in 1785–1786. In June 1785, the Lodge voted that "there be no Publick Festival" while in December, it was "voted unanimously that this Lodge will not celebrate the Festival of St. John the Baptist." In June 1786, the motion to celebrate the feast was "Negatived" and in December, it was again concluded not to hold the festival. The feasts are not mentioned in 1787 or 1788.[93]

Feast day festivals were again held from 1789 through the early 1790s. Revere was involved with the arrangements for every celebration and also served regularly on the follow-up committees after the festivals were over. Although Revere was actively involved with the Grand Lodge throughout the 1780s, he was an officeholder for only a portion of the decade. Having served as Senior Grand Warden from December 1779 until December 1783, he was chosen as Deputy Grand Master in 1783, and held the position throughout 1784. At the next election, in June 1785, Revere was not chosen for an office. At this time, Paul Revere was actively involved with Rising States Lodge and was an officer in that Lodge throughout most of the decade. In 1790, Revere was again awarded with a position in the Grand Lodge—that of Deputy Grand Master—being re-elected in June 1791.[94]

In the early 1780s, the Grand Lodge was meeting at Masons' Hall, or the Green Dragon Tavern, owned by St. Andrew's Lodge. By March 1784, after the split with St. Andrew's, the Grand Lodge voted "that a Committee of three be Chose to see if this Grand Lodge Can be better Accommodated with a room." After 1784, meetings were held most frequently at the Bunch of Grapes Tavern in State Street, also referred to as the "House of Brother Marstion," where Rising States Lodge also met. By 1790, meetings were regularly held at Concert Hall, which was located on the corner of Court and Hanover Streets. In March 1791, it was "motioned by Worshipfull Brother Revere that the Grand Lodge in future meet on the first Monday in June, September, December + March." The motion was seconded and passed.[95]

As the decade of the 1780s drew to a close, a movement was beginning which would secure and strengthen the institution of Freemasonry in the State of Massachusetts by uniting Boston's two Grand Lodges. Through committee work, Paul Revere participated in the process which resulted in the union of St. John's Grand Lodge and the Massachusetts Grand Lodge in March 1792. Five years earlier, in March 1787, a committee was raised to "confer with the other Grand Lodge [St. John's] in order if possible to obtain a Union among Masons, respecting the Choice of a Grand Master." Paul Revere was included on this five man committee. The following month, a second committee was formed for the purpose of writing to the Lodges in the jurisdiction "to obtain their Sentiments upon the subject" of a union. The matter did not surface again until 1791, by which time Paul Revere was serving as Deputy Grand Master. At this time, a committee was appointed "to Confer with the Officers of St. John's Grand Lodge upon the subject of a compleat Masonic Union throughout this Commonwealth." Paul Revere was also on this committee. When the union finally occurred three months later, on March 19, 1792, the Massachusetts Grand Lodge was prepared. On March 5, the Lodge had read and agreed to a "Constitution + laws for associating the St. John's + the Massachusetts Grand Lodges . . . + accepted by St. John's Grand Lodge." A list of prospective officers was prepared and Paul Revere was chosen as one of seven Electors "agreeable to Constitution" who would meet with Electors from St. John's Grand Lodge.

Although Revere was not proposed as an officer, he served on a committee to thank the Grand Master for his services, and was also one of three masons directed to "adjust all the Accots of the Grand Lodge" and see to it that "all records & masonic papers with furnature + regalia of this G. Lodge be collected and . . . deliver'd to the Grand Master Elect." It was then "voted that this Grand Lodge be dissolved." With the union, the new Grand Lodge was called "The Grand Lodge of the Most Ancient and Honourable Society of Free and Accepted Masons for the Commonwealth of Massachusetts."[96]

IX

GRAND MASTER PAUL REVERE

The culmination of Paul Revere's thirty-four years as a Freemason came in 1794 when he attained the most prominent and prestigious position in the State—that of Grand Master of the newly-formed Massachusetts Grand Lodge. By 1784, ten years earlier, Revere had already risen as high as Deputy Grand Master, with his appointment under John Warren. He again served as Deputy Grand Master under Moses M. Hayes in 1791–1792. Revere was finally chosen as Grand Master at the annual election of officers on December 8, 1794, a position he held through 1797. According to the Constitution of the Grand Lodge, the Grand Master was to be elected by a ballot at large with "every voter writing the candidate he thinks best qualified." The brother who had two-thirds of the votes cast was elected Grand Master. Ironically, Paul Revere was not the first choice of the assembled brethren for Grand Master in 1794. John Warren, brother of the late Joseph Warren, was again chosen but he "declined accepting the Chair." The Grand Lodge

> . . . then proceeded to another choice, when it appeared that the Rt. Worshipful Paul Revere was chosen: he not being present, a committee of three . . . were appointed to wait on Brother P. Revere to know whether he would accept the appointment; which committee reported his acceptance.

Paul Revere's installation as Grand Master took place on December 12, 1794 at Concert Hall, where "the Most Worshipful John Cutler, then, in Ample Form, installed the Grand Master and placed him in the chair of Solomon and invested him with his proper jewels." Duly installed, Revere appointed his Deputy, Deacons, Stewards, Grand Marshall and Sword Bearer, and invested them with their jewels. According to Lodge minutes, "a procession was then formed and the Brethren, in their proper order, paid their usual salutes and congratulations."[97]

While Revere was Grand Master, the Grand Lodge held four quarterly communications on the second Mondays of December, March,

June and September. Lodge meetings were regularly held at Concert Hall. Paul Revere attended every meeting during his three years as Master and the fraternity expanded energetically under his direction. The celebration of feast days also continued. In June 1795, Revere served on a committee to arrange the Feast of St. John the Baptist, complete with festivities at Concert Hall and a procession to and from the Chapel Church. Revere also seems to have been the first Grand Master to appoint a Lodge Chaplain, as it was voted on December 12, 1796 that "The Most Worshipful Grand Master be authorized at every annual meeting to appoint a Grand Chaplain, whose duty it shall be to attend the Grand Lodge and perform such clerical duties as shall be assigned him."[98]

While Grand Master, Paul Revere also continued the distribution of the volume of *Constitutions*. The book was compiled in 1792, due to the union between the Massachusetts Grand Lodge and St. John's Grand Lodge. The book of *Constitutions* was a compilation of masonic history, charges, addresses, constitutions, laws and songs entitled *The Constitutions of the Ancient and Honorable Fraternity of Free and Accepted Masons*. In December 1792, the Grand Lodge thanked the committee which had been appointed to compile the volume "for the very eminent services thereby rendered in that important work." Paul Revere was one of thirteen masons who served on the committee (see Illustration 6), under the direction of the Reverend Thaddeus Mason Harris. The Grand Lodge intended to send a copy of the book to every Lodge in the State, as well as presenting the volume to all new Lodges chartered. According to Revere, the constitutions were "calculated with so much pains, for the benifit of the Craft, having upon all occasions, recourse to their excellent Charges, & regulations therein contained . . ." After Revere's election in 1795, the "Book of Constitutions, handsomely bound" was also presented to the Massachusetts Historical Society and the Boston Library Society. In September 1796, on behalf of the Library Society, the Reverend John Elliot "desired to wait upon Col. Revere . . . to thank him for his politeness and beg him to transmit their grateful thanks to the Grand Lodge." Revere must have had a sincere interest in the rules and regulations which kept the fraternity running smoothly, as he often served on committees to revise masonic rules and bylaws. In 1797, he served on a committee to "revise the Constitutions of the Grand Lodge." He also wrote the "charges" which were used in the installation of officers while he was Grand Master.[99]

Since the primary responsibility of the Massachusetts Grand Lodge was to charter new Lodges and supervise the Lodges within its jurisdiction, much Grand Lodge activity was devoted to seeing that the Lodges were properly organized and legally conducted. As Grand Master, Paul Revere chartered at least twenty-three new Lodges within Massachusetts and Maine (see Appendix 4), as well as serving on committees dealing with Lodge problems. In December 1796, Revere was one of a three man committee raised to confer with a committee from Columbian Lodge "and report their doings at the next Quarterly meeting." In March 1797, Paul Revere was on a committee appointed to write to the Lodges at Marblehead and Nantucket. Several months later, on August 27, Revere wrote a personal letter to Samuel Barrett at the Union Lodge in Nantucket informing him that "except your Lodge send their Charter to, And paid this dues to the Massachusetts Grand Lodge, you would not be received by them, or acknowledged as a regular, constituted Lodge." Revere informed him that according to a "general regulation," any Lodge "who does not pay their dues to, and are Represented in, the Grand Lodge of the State where the Lodge is held, shall be viewed as a Clandestine Lodge + treated as such." As Grand Master, Paul Revere felt it was his "duty to represent to you your situation, as a Lodge, not doubting, you will take such steps as Free & Accepted Masons ought to . . ." The Union Lodge was originally chartered on May 27, 1771. The Lodge replied in early September that they had raised a committee to look into the matter. Union Lodge might have violated a resolve issued by the Grand Lodge two years earlier in 1795, which specified that

> when any Lodge in this Jurisdiction is not represented in Grand Lodge and is in arrears for a longer period than twelve months it shall be considered as having relinquished its connection with this Grand Lodge and not having a regular Masonic standing in the Commonwealth.[100]

Paul Revere was concerned not only with the proper conduct of the Lodges, but also with the quality of masonic candidates. While Grand Master, he wrote the ceremony for constituting a new Lodge, in which he instructed the officers to

> . . . carefully enquire into the Character of all Candidates . . . and reccommend none to the Master, who in your oppinion, are unworthy of the priviledges, & advantages of Masonry, Keeping the CYNIC, far from the Antient Fraternity, were Harmony is obstructed by the Superstitious, & Morose . . .

Ten years after he served as Grand Master, Paul Revere's concern about candidates was still clear. He wrote that "it is too much the practice of Lodges to admit the 'worthless and profane', to polute our 'hallowed Temple.' 'Caution' and jealousy, with respect to Candidates, cannot be too much impressed on all Lodges." In February 1797, Revere served on a committee of three to draft a resolve against the improper admission of candidates, when it came to his attention that persons who were rejected in one Lodge would "afterwards apply to another Lodge within the jurisdiction and gain admittance." As Grand Master, Revere had the authority to prevent the "worthless and profane" from joining masonic Lodges within his jurisdiction. In 1797, Revere brought charges against Harmonic Lodge for directly violating his authority in this respect. According to Revere's charges, the Lodge made "a number of persons masons, without handing their names to the Grand Master for his approbation." They also made a number of persons masons "all of them persons to whom the Grand Master had refused his approbation." Lastly, on the same evening, they made "nine persons masons, some of whom had not stood the usual time on the books, and without having first obtained a dispensation from the Grand Master for that purpose." On June 28, 1797, Paul Revere and a majority of the Grand Lodge voted to "vacate" the charter of Harmonic Lodge.[101]

The most memorable event during Revere's term as Grand Master, and a high point for Massachusetts Freemasonry, was the laying of the cornerstone of the new State House on Boston Common, July 4th, 1795. In the great tradition of the ancient stonemasons and master builders, the Grand Lodge of Massachusetts was invited by Governor Samuel Adams to assist in the ceremony, which was also conducted with a full masonic procession. The new State House was designed by Charles Bulfinch, erected by master builder and Freemason Amos Lincoln, and before long had its dome sheathed with sheet copper rolled in Paul Revere's copper mill. The event was commemorated by an inscribed silver plate placed beneath the cornerstone. The inscription read:

> This Corner-Stone intended for the use of the Legislature and Executive Branches of Government of the Commonwealth of Massachusetts was laid by His Excellency Samuel Adams, Esqr. Governor of said Commonwealth assisted by the Most Worshipful Paul Revere, Grand Master; and the Right Worshipful William Scollay, Deputy Grand Master; The Grand Wardens and Brethren of the Grand Lodge of Massachusetts on the 4th Day of July 1795 being the 20th Anniversary of American Independence.[102]

The procession was lengthy and must have been an impressive once. After gathering at the Representative Chamber, the participants proceeded to the Old South Meeting House to hear an oration, after which they proceeded to the new State House site in the following masonic order. The Independent Fusiliers with "Martial Musick" led the procession, followed by two Tylers. Then came the cornerstone, placed on a truck decorated with ribbons, drawn by fifteen white horses. The stone was followed by the Operative masons who would help secure it in place. Then came the Speculative masons—the Grand Marshal and Stewards with staves, the Entered Apprentices and

Fellow Crafts, and three Master Masons carrying the square, level and plumb rule respectively. Next came three Stewards, bearing corn, wine and oil, and the Master Masons. Lodge officers wearing jewels, Lodge Past Masters and the Grand Tyler with a cushion and Bible were all followed by a "Band of Music". Next proceeded the Grand Lodge officers—the Grand Deacons with wands, the Grand Treasurer and Secretary, the Past Grand Wardens, the Senior and Junior Grand Wardens, the Past Deputy Grand Masters and the Past Grand Masters. The Reverend Clergy were next, and then came Paul Revere, Grand Master, attended by the Deputy Grand Master, Grand Stewards and Grand Sword-Bearer. The State officials followed—the Sheriff of Suffolk, the agents of the Commonwealth and finally his Excellency Governor Samuel Adams. Adams was followed by the Lieutenant Governor, the Assistant and Quarter Master General, the Honorable Council and Members of the Legislature. Clergy and "Strangers of Distinction" brought up the rear.[103]

To this assembled crowd, Paul Revere delivered the following brief address:

Worshipfull Brethren, I congratulate you on this auspicious day;—when the Arts and Sciences are establishing themselves in our happy Country, a Country distinguished from the rest of the World, by being a Government of Laws.—Where Liberty has found a Safe and Secure abode,—and where her Sons are determined to support and protect her.

Brethren, we are called this day by our Venerable + patriotic Governor, his Excellency Samuel Adams, to Assist him in laying the Corner Stone of a Building to be erected for the use of the Legislature and Executive branches of Government of this Commonwealth. May we my Brethren, so Square our Actions thro life as to shew to the *World of Mankind*, that we mean to live within the *Compass* of Good Citizens that we wish to Stand upon a Level with them that when we part we may be admitted into that Temple where Reigns Silence & peace. (See Illustration 7.)

After the Operative masons prepared the cornerstone, it was laid into place by Governor Samuel Adams, assisted by Grand Master Paul Revere and the Deputy Grand Master. Beneath the stone, Revere had placed "a number of gold, silver and copper coins, and a silver plate" which bore the inscription. The ceremony was concluded to the roar of cannon and the cheering crowd.[104]

The ceremony on Boston Common was reminiscent of a similar event which took place only two years earlier in Washington. On September 18, 1793, George Washington, in a full masonic ceremony, laid the cornerstone for the National Capital Building. Masons throughout the "thirteen United North American States" felt deep respect and brotherhood for their beloved leader and fellow mason.

As early as 1780, it was even suggested that George Washington be appointed a Grand Master General over all American masons. This idea was conveyed to the Massachusetts Grand Lodge by the Grand Lodge of Pennsylvania, which thought it "Expedient to Make Choice of a Grand Master General for the Thirteen United American States," for which position "they had Nominated his Excellancy General George Washington." The Massachusetts Grand Lodge referred the suggestion to committees, one of which included Paul Revere, which wrote to the constituent Lodges for their opinions on the subject. After some debate, by January 1781, the Massachusetts Grand Lodge reached a decision, offering the following justification.

> As this Grand Lodge have not been Acquainted with the Opinion of the Various Grand Lodges in the United States, Respecting the Choice of a Grand Master General, and the Circumstances of Our Public Affairs Making it Impossible we should at Present, obtain their Sentiments upon it, Therefore Voted, that any determination upon the Subject cannot with the Propriety and Justice due to the Craft at large be made by This Grand Lodge untill a GENERAL PEACE shall happily take place thro' the Continent.[105]

Although the Massachusetts Grand Lodge temporarily rejected the idea of a Grand Master General, its affection for George Washington remained unshaken. The Lodge dedicated its volume of *Constitutions* to him, and promptly sent a copy to "our most beloved Brother George Washington" with a "suitable address" in December 1792. Washington thanked his Massachusetts Brethren with "all those emotions of gratitude," certain that the masons and their publication would "convince mankind that the Grand object of Masonry is to promote the happiness of the human race." In March 1797, when George Washington retired from public life, the Massachusetts masons voted that a "committee be appointed to draft an Address to be presented to our Illustrious Brother George Washington Esqr." A committee of five, led by Grand Master Paul Revere, was appointed. The letter, prepared by June 1797, was signed by Revere and three other Lodge officers. The masons hoped that after his busy public life, Washington might enjoy a "calm retirement" and take comfort in the masonic fraternity, which would afford him "all the relief of tranquility, the harmony of peace and the refreshment of pleasure." The masons hoped that through Washington's "encouragement, assistance and patronage, the Craft will attain its highest ornament, perfection and praise."[106]

Paul Revere's public life as a Freemason was also coming to an end. By late 1797, Revere had served for three years as Grand Master. It was the last major masonic office he would hold. As new officers were chosen on December 11, 1797, Revere "was then pleased to address the Grand Lodge in a fraternal manner in which his abilities in the masonic art were eminently displayed." Revere viewed this masonic election as a farewell. He knew that, having served as Grand Master for three years, he was ineligible for re-election, according to the Constitution, but he could say with pride that there were "upwards of forty" Lodges within the jurisdiction, most of which were represented and paid dues. This nearly doubled the number of twenty-two Lodges which were in the jurisdiction after the two Grand Lodges united in 1792, each Grand Lodge having brought eleven Lodges to the union.[107]

After three productive years, Paul Revere's address reveals his contentment with the past, as well as the issues which concerned him for the future of masonry. The Union Lodge at Nantucket still had not complied with the regulations, but he was confident that it would do so if his successor "provided a little attention." Revere also encouraged a "free correspondence" between masonic Lodges in the United States and abroad. The Lodges of England and Nova Scotia had already extended a cordial correspondence with America, and Revere thought the same should be done with "Quebeck," as a means of "securing the friendship of that Body of Masons against those persons who may wish to make inovations in Masonry." With just a little attention to correspondence, Revere was certain "that we shall soon have the pleasure to Communicate with every G^d Lodge thro' the Globe." Revere was also concerned with the "necessity of subordination among Masons," hoping that the Lodges would conduct themselves according to the old traditions. He encouraged "a carefull attention to our Constitution; that you never suffer the antient landmarks to be removed; that a Strict attention be paid to every Lodge under this jurisdiction" so that "they be not suffered to break thro, or, treat with neglect any of the regulations of the Grand Lodge." Revere also recommended that "a Committee be raised to form regulations for the disposal of Charity, or any other thing that will add to the happiness of Masons." A committee was immediately appointed "to take into consideration the recommendations made by the most worshipful Grand Master . . ." during his final address.[108]

As Paul Revere left the highest masonic office in the State, he professed great hopes for the future. According to Revere, Freemasonry "is now in a more flourishing situation than it has been for Ages" and there is "no quarter of the Globe but accknowledges its Philantrophy . . ." He felt it was "the greatest happiness" of his life

> to have presided in the G^d Lodge at a time when FreeMasonry has attained so great a heighth that its benign influence has spread its self to every part of the Globe + shines with more resplendent rays, than it hath since the days when King Solomon imployed our immortal G^d Master to build the Temple.

Revere began his address with an apology, assuring his masonic brethren that he "endeavoured to pay every attention to what I esteemed my duty," adding that "I have never omitted to do one act that appeared to be for the good of the Craft" but "if I have done what I ought not to have done, you must impute it to my head & not to my heart." Revere closed his address by extending to his fellow masons "my most sincere + hearty thanks for your Candor, and assistance," since it was "owing to your kind attention and assistance that I have been enabled to do the little good which has been done . . ." He encouraged his brethren to "continue the same kindness to all my Successors in office . . ." On December 27, 1797, Revere installed the new Grand Master and officially ended his three year term. The Lodge voted that thanks be given "to our most Worshipful Master Paul Revere, Esqr. for his eminent service rendered this Grand Lodge while in the Chair of Solomon."[109]

Paul Revere remained active with the Grand Lodge after 1797 although he no longer held a masonic office. As a Past Grand Master, he attended meetings regularly and served on Lodge committees. Revere served on nearly every committee raised at the suggestion of his final masonic address of December 11. Upon receiving a letter from the Grand Lodge of England, Paul Revere was included on the "committee of correspondence" raised to draft a reply. On January 17, 1798, he worked on a committee to procure a plate for granting certificates, and another dealing with the distribution of charity. Also in January, the masons considered revising their *Constitutions,* again under the direction of the Reverend Thaddeus Harris. Revere was on the committees appointed to examine the copy before it went to the press, and also to compensate the Reverend for his work. In December 1798, a committee was formed "to consider the State of Masonry in this Commonwealth" and "to report their opinion of the expediency of erecting more Lodges." Paul Revere was included, as well as assisting with a letter of protest to Columbian Lodge. Revere also served on a committee at the June meeting, 1799. By December 1799, a committee was formed to meet with St. Andrew's Lodge "on the propriety of their acknowledging the jurisdiction of this Grand Lodge," a measure considered "highly essential to the fair reputation of the masonic character in the opinion of our country." St. Andrew's Lodge still considered itself to be within the jurisdiction of the Grand Lodge of Scotland. Paul Revere served on this committee. He was also chosen proxy for Holmes' Hole Lodge at Martha's Vineyard at the meeting of December 9, 1799.[110]

X

GEORGE WASHINGTON—DEATH AND MOURNING

Five days later, an event occurred which shocked the new nation. In 1797, Paul Revere and his committee had written a letter to George Washington, sending not only good wishes for his retirement, but also the

> earnest prayer, that when your light shall be no more visible in this earthly Temple, you may be raised to the All Perfect Lodge above, be seated on the right of the Supreme Architect of the Universe, and receive the refreshment your labors have merited.

The death of Washington came suddenly on December 14, 1799, less than three years later. Expressions of grief and respect were universal. Bells tolled, cannon roared, flags flew at half-mast and business stopped. Mourning badges quickly appeared. The Grand Lodge recommended "a crepe with a new blue ribband," and ladies wore arm badges with the initials G. W. Every sermon from every pulpit was devoted to Washington. The Reverend William Bentley of Salem was asked to deliver the eulogy on Washington in that town, and he was also the Grand Chaplain of the Grand Lodge of Massachusetts. Bentley observed that there were "preparations everywhere for Eulogies and funeral processions . . . The same tokens of respect prevail everywhere." By January 12, 1800, Salem alone had appropriated six thousand dollars for "funeral and other honours," which the town agreed to pay through taxes as a tribute to Washington.[111]

Boston held its funeral procession on January 8, 1800, but the Massachusetts Grand Lodge did not participate. Instead, it held a special meeting on January 8 and voted to hold its own funeral procession on February 11, including every Lodge within its jurisdiction. It even invited St. Andrew's Lodge. A committee was appointed to arrange the procession and choose an orator, while another committee was raised to write to Washington's widow "condoling with her in her heavy affliction," and requesting "a lock of her deceased husband's hair to be preserved in a Golden Urn, with the jewels and regalia of the Grand Lodge." Paul Revere served on both committees. The latter committee also drafted a letter of condolence to the several Grand Lodges in the United States.[112]

On February 11, 1800, sixteen hundred masons met in Boston to commemorate George Washington's death in a masonic funeral service. The ceremony began at eight o'clock with the tolling of bells, followed by a Grand Procession at eleven o'clock. The procession was not unlike that which attended the cornerstone ceremony five years earlier, but evidence of mourning was abundant. The procession was led by the two Grand Pursuivants on "elegant white horses properly caparisoned" bearing an "eliptical mourning Arch (14 feet in the clear)" with a sacred text in silver letters. The masons followed in their proper order, each with a sprig of cassia and a mourning badge. The Grand Lodge officers were dressed in full mourning "with white scarfs and weeds." Appropriate officers carried mourning wands and staves "suitably shrouded."[113]

The central focus of the procession was an urn and pedestal, carried by six pall-bearers dressed in full mourning. Paul Revere was one of the pall-bearers who carried

> A Pedestal covered with a Pall, the escutcheon of which were characteristic drawings, on satin, of Faith, Hope and Charity. The Pedestal beside the Urn, which was upwards of three feet in length, and which contained a relic of the Illustrious deceased, bore also a representation of the Genius of Masonry, weeping on the Urn, and other suitable emblems . . .

This was not the "Golden Urn" mentioned in the letter to Mrs. Washington, but the "whole [was] of white marble composition." The relic of George Washington contained in the urn could have been the lock of hair, which Mrs. Washington sent to the Grand Lodge in late January. The white urn was inscribed "Sacred to the Memory of Brother GEORGE WASHINGTON; raised to the ALL-PERFECT LODGE DEC. 14, 5799.—Ripe in years and full of glory." The complete procession assembled at the old South Meeting House, where they heard prayers, odes and the eulogy delivered by Brother Timothy Bigelow. The eulogy contained "a blaze of chaste portraits of the Illustrious Washington, drawn as a warrior, a statesman, a citizen, a Christian, and a Mason . . ." After the Benediction was given and a final dirge sung, the group moved to the Stone Chapel where the Reverend William Bentley performed a funeral service which was "accomodated to the Solemn Occasion." After being assembled "above seven hours," the procession parted after five o'clock, when the masons "returned to the State House unclothed and separated."[114]

After the procession was disbanded, Revere invited the Reverend

William Bentley to supper, an event which Bentley noted in his diary. He dined with a "select company" that included Revere, Isaiah Thomas, Jacob Perkins and a Mr. Reynolds. Isaiah Thomas and Revere had served together as masons for many years. According to Bentley, Isaiah Thomas was "the Father of the Press in New England" who "carried the extent of the Business beyond any man in America." Revere produced many engravings for works that rolled off the presses of Isaiah Thomas. Jacob Perkins of Newburyport was "eminent for his Mechanic genius" as well as "for his excellent medals, in a great variety, of our General Washington." With his inventions, he had already revolutionized the making of paper money and the manufacture of nails. The third member of this "select company" was Mr. Reynolds, known for his work in artificial stone. It was he who fashioned the "admirable Urn and weeping innocent, which was displayed with so great success by the Brethren for the public admiration." He showed the company several busts of Washington which were "peculiarly expressive of the true countenance of our departed general." Bentley referred to Revere as "an antient Past G. Master." Both men were born in Boston's North End and it was Bentley's father who had rowed Paul Revere across the Charles River on the night of April 18, 1775, when he embarked upon his now famous ride to Lexington. Bentley had retained his contact with Revere through the masons and often visited the North End when he was in Boston, stopping at the foundry which Revere had established on Lynn Street in 1788. It was there that Revere cast the first church bell in Boston in 1792. Bentley also ordered a bell "892 lbs. without a stock or tongue" from this "enterprising mechanic" in 1801.[115]

The mourning for Washington continued at least until February 22, 1800, which was designated by Congress as "the day of National Sorrow and Public Grief." William Bentley noted that on Sunday, February 23, he performed his "eighth Service upon the death of Washington" which finished "the public mourning of the Congregation." Once the services and processions were completed, it remained to dispose of the funeral regalia. A Grand Lodge comittee appointed to find "some suitable place for the deposit of the Urn and regalia used in the procession on the 11th of February last" made its report on June 9, 1800. The committee reported that Paul Revere had "received them into his house and kindly offered to take charge of them," which the committee was more than happy to have him do on behalf of the Grand Lodge. The regalia consisted of the artificial white marble urn which was made by Mr. Reynolds "and its appendages." By this time, Revere had moved from his wooden house on North Square to a three story brick building on Charter Street, several blocks away. Revere housed the urn on Charter Street for many years. In 1809, a Grand Lodge committee examined the possibility of depositing the regalia in Masons' Hall, "directly over the chair of the M.W.

Grand Master." The committee visited Revere's house and reported that "the most scrupulous care has been observed in the preservation of the urn and its appendages . . ." The Grand Lodge voted its thanks to Revere for his devoted care of the urn, and requested that he "permit them to remain under his protection, untill the Grand Lodge shall have it in their power—Otherwise to dispose of them."[116]

The lock of Washington's hair was also destined to have a new home. The original letter to Mrs. Washington had directed that a "Golden Urn be prepared as a deposit for a lock of hair, an *invaluable* relique of the Hero and the Patriot . . ." The committee, which investigated a "suitable place" for the white urn in June 1800, also reported that "the procuring the Gold Urn is in great forwardness." Several months later, the committee appointed "to procure the Golden Urn" reported that a "suitable inscription" was being devised. The end result was a small gold urn, made by Paul Revere, which was later mounted upon a mahogany pedestal that also served as a storage cabinet. (See Illustration 8.) The urn was 3⅞ inches high, while the pedestal measured 6½ inches tall by 3¼ inches square, with an interior lined in blue velvet. The urn was simply inscribed "This URN incloses a Lock of HAIR/of the Immortal WASHINGTON/PRESENTED JANUARY 27, 1800/to the Massachusetts GRAND LODGE/ by HIS amiable WIDOW./ Born Feby 11th, 1732/Ob^t Decr 14, 1799." Beneath the urn's cover, the lock of hair was secured under glass. Paul Revere was a logical choice to craft the urn. Although he had expanded into other business ventures after the Revolution, the quality of his work as a goldsmith was unmatched. He had also been on the committee that wrote the letter of condolence to Mrs. Washington, the same committee which suggested the creation of a "Golden Urn." Unlike the white urn, which remained in Revere's care for years, the gold urn was kept with the jewels and regalia of the Grand Lodge where it was, and still is, "cherished as the most precious jewel in the cabinet."[117]

XI

ILLUSTRATIONS

Illustration 1: Presented on cover with description on copyright page.

Illustration 2: Green Dragon Tavern, 1773. Pen and ink drawing with water color wash by Boston portrait painter John Johnson. The Tavern was purchased by St. Andrew's Lodge on March 31, 1764. According to Lodge tradition, plans for the "Boston Tea Party" were made at the Tavern. Courtesy, American Antiquarian Society.

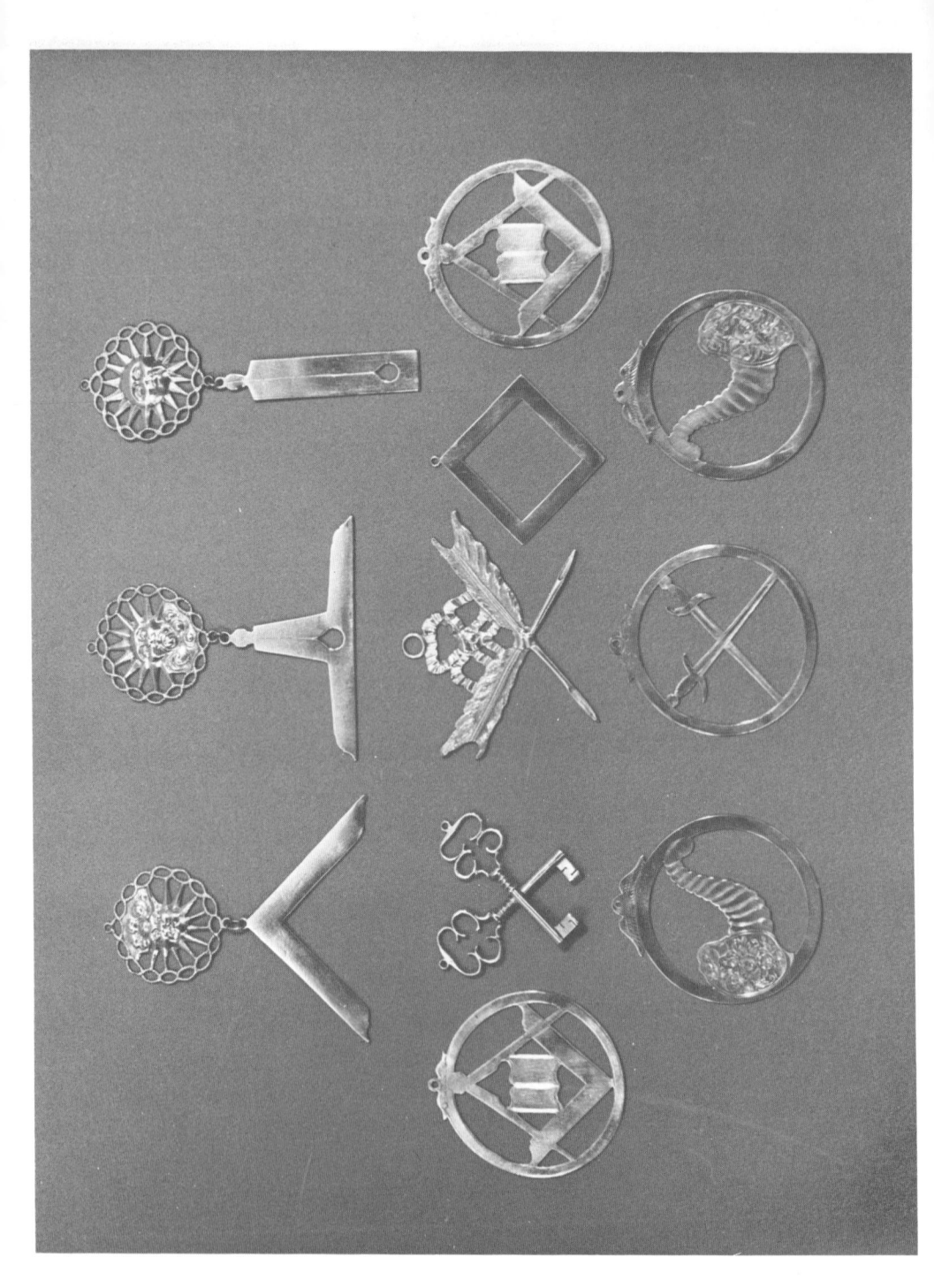

Illustration 3: Masonic Officer's Jewels made of silver by Paul Revere for Washington Lodge, 1796. Since masonic symbolism was relatively standardized, probable identification and officer usage is as follows: Top row, left to right: The Square—Master; Level—Senior Warden; Plumb—Junior Warden; Middle row, left to right: The Square and Compasses—Junior and Senior Deacons; Crossed Keys—Treasurer; Crossed Quills—Secretary; Use unknown for diamond-shaped jewel; Botton row, left to right: Horns of Plenty—Stewards; Crossed Swords—Tyler. Courtesy, Museum of Our National Heritage.

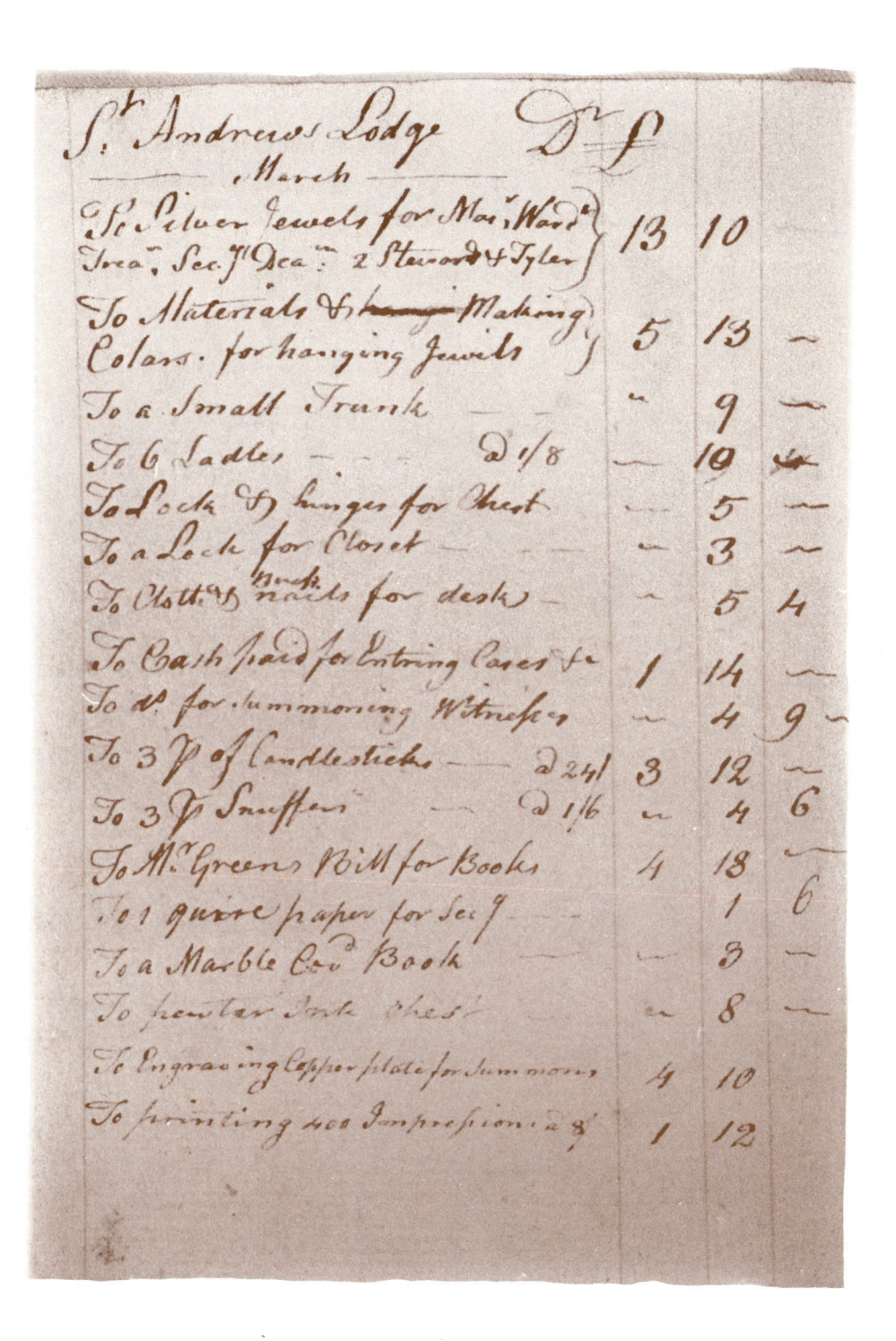

St Andrews Lodge	Dr £		
March			
To Silver Jewels for Mar. Ward. Trea., Sec., 3 Dea., 2 Steward & Tyler	13	10	
To Materials & Making Colars. for hanging Jewels	5	13	—
To a Small Trunk	—	9	—
To 6 Ladles @ 1/8	—	10	—
To Lock & hinges for Chest	—	5	—
To a Lock for Closet	—	3	—
To Cloth & nails for desk	—	5	4
To Cash paid for Entring Cases &c	1	14	—
To do. for Summoning Witnesses	—	4	9
To 3 p. of Candlesticks @ 24/	3	12	—
To 3 p. Snuffers @ 1/6	—	4	6
To Mr Greens Bill for Books	4	18	—
To 1 quire paper for Sec.y	—	1	6
To a Marble Cov.d Book	—	3	—
To pewter Ink chest	—	8	—
To Engraving Copper plate for Summons	4	10	—
To printing 400 Impressions @ 8/	1	12	—

Illustration 4: Page From Paul Revere's Record Book, kept while Revere was Treasurer of Rising States Lodge (originally called St. Andrew's Lodge). The Lodge was founded in early 1784, with Revere as the first Treasurer. This page is from March 1784 and records the purchase of many Lodge necessities. Photographed with permission of the Grand Lodge of Masons in Massachusetts, A.F. & A.M.

Illustration 5: Masonic Seal for Rising States Lodge, c. 1784. Silver. Possibly made by Paul Revere. Photographed with permission of the Grand Lodge of Masons in Massachusetts, A.F. & A.M.

Sanction.

To all the **Fraternity** *of* **Free** *and* **Accepted Masons.**

WHEREAS the GRAND LODGE of our Most Ancient and Honourable Society, for the Commonwealth of MASSACHUSETTS, at a Special Meeting on the evening of the second day of April, 5792, did regularly appoint our worthy Brethren *John Warren, Moses M. Hays, Paul Revere, Aaron Dexter, William Scollay, Thaddeus M. Harris, John Lowell, Samuel Dunn, James Jackson, Samuel Barret, William Little, Samuel Parkman,* and *John Flemming,* a COMMITTEE, with full power to " consider and compile a BOOK of CONSTITUTIONS, containing all things necessary for the use of the Fraternity ;" and did also resolve that the said Book should be " *Published under the* SANCTION *of the* GRAND MASTER *and* GRAND WARDENS :"

WE, the Subscribers, having duly examined the following work as reported by the Committee, DO hereby, in behalf of the Grand Lodge, RECOM-

Illustration 6: Sanction page from *The Constitutions of the Ancient and Honorable Fraternity of Free and Accepted Masons* published by the Massachusetts Grand Lodge, 1792. Paul Revere was on the Committee which compiled the volume. Courtesy of the Trustees of the Boston Public Library.

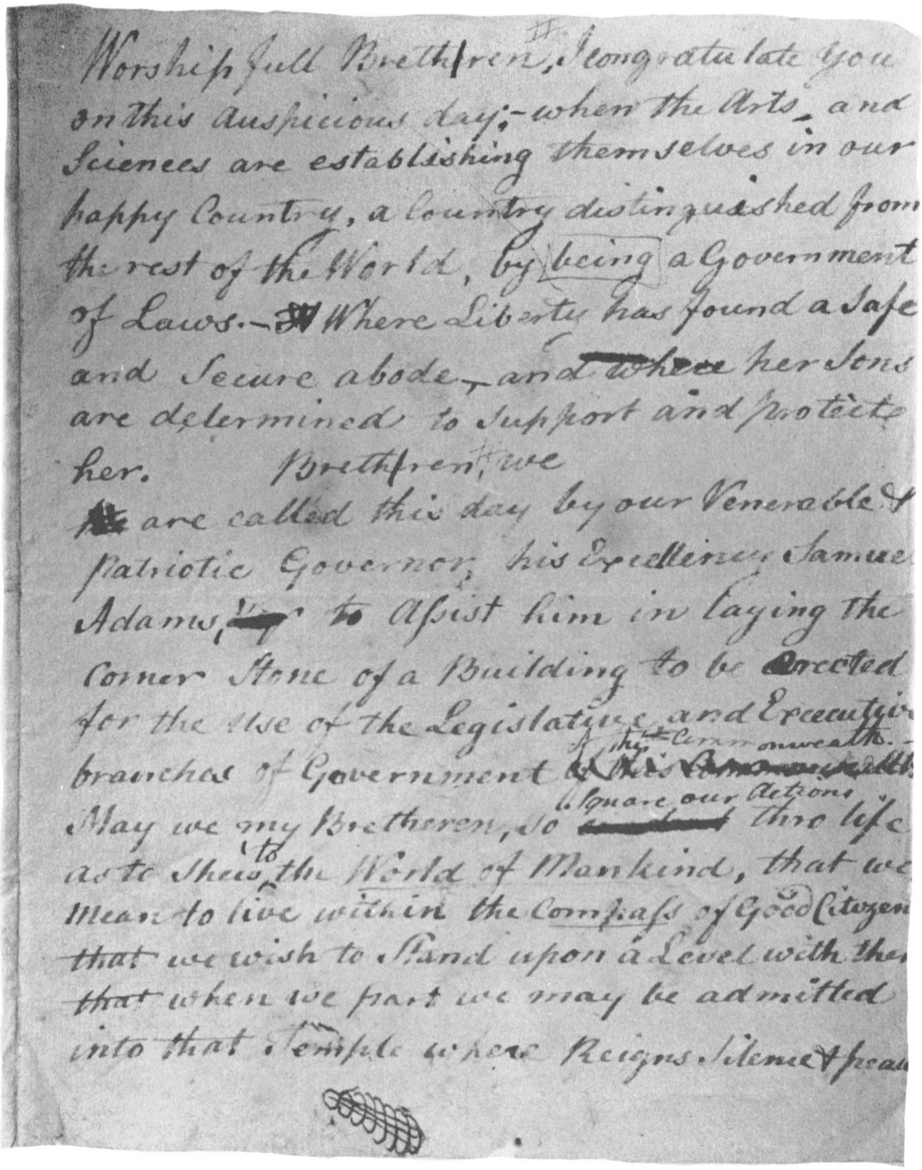

Worshipfull Brethren, I congratulate you
on this auspicious day;—when the Arts, and
Sciences are establishing themselves in our
happy Country, a Country distinguished from
the rest of the World, by being a Government
of Laws.— Where Liberty has found a Safe
and Secure abode,— and ~~where~~ her Sons
are determined to Support and protecte
her. Brethren, we
are called this day by our Venerable &
patriotic Governor, his Excellency Samuel
Adams, to Assist him in laying the
Corner Stone of a Building to be erected
for the Use of the Legislative and Executive
branches of Government of the Commonwealth ~~& this Commonwealth~~
May we my Bretheren, so Square our Actions ~~conduct~~ thro life
as to Shew to the World of Mankind, that we
Mean to live within the Compass of Good Citizens
that we wish to Stand upon a Level with them
that when we part we may be admitted
into that Temple where Reigns Silence & peace

Illustration 7: Speech delivered by Paul Revere during a masonic ceremony for the laying of the cornerstone of the New State House, Boston, July 4, 1795, while Revere was Grand Master of the Massachusetts Grand Lodge. Photographed with permission of the Grand Lodge of Masons in Massachusetts, A.F. & A.M.

Illustration 8: Gold Urn made by Paul Revere for the Massachusetts Grand Lodge after the death of George Washington to preserve a lock of his hair, 1800–1801. Courtesy, Grand Lodge of Masons in Massachusetts, A.F. & A.M.

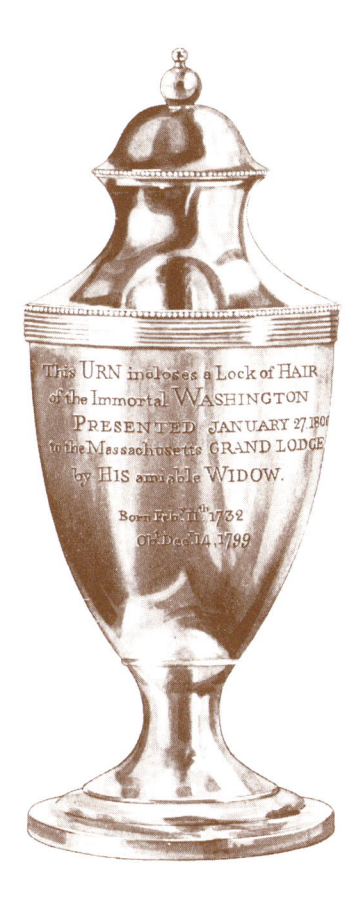

The Columbian Lodge to Paul
Revere and Son ———————— Dr.

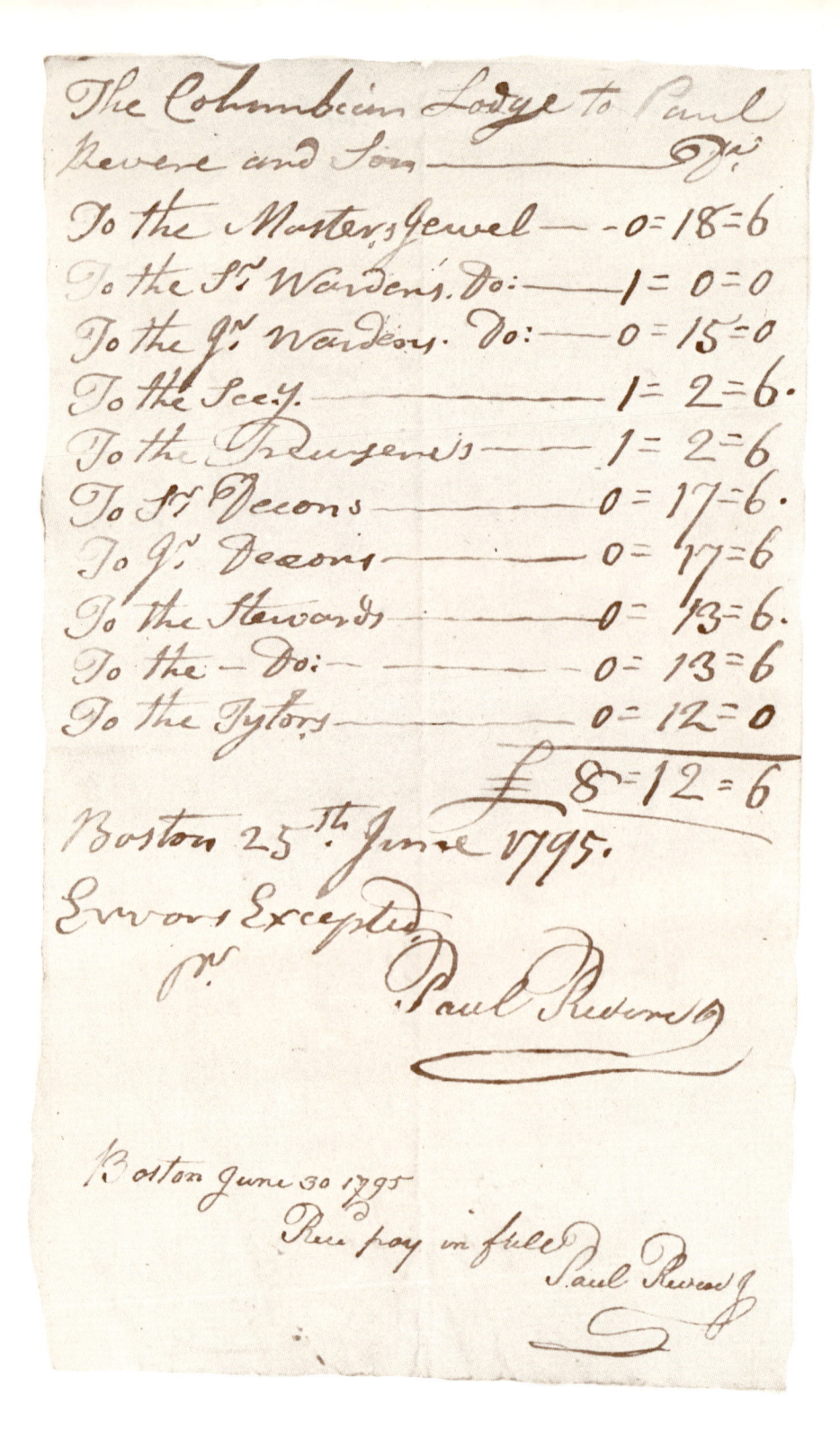

To the Masters Jewel	0 = 18 = 6
To the Sr. Wardens Do:	1 = 0 = 0
To the Jr. Wardens Do:	0 = 15 = 0
To the Secy.	1 = 2 = 6
To the Treasurers	1 = 2 = 6
To Sr. Decons	0 = 17 = 6
To Jr. Decons	0 = 17 = 6
To the Stewards	0 = 13 = 6
To the — Do:	0 = 13 = 6
To the Tylors	0 = 12 = 0
£	8 = 12 = 6

Boston 25th June 1795.
Errors Excepted
pr.
Paul Revere

Boston June 30 1795
Recd pay in full
Paul Revere

Illustration 9: Receipt from Paul Revere to Columbian Lodge, Boston, for a set of Masonic Officer's Jewels, June 25, 1795. Courtesy, Museum of Our National Heritage.

Illustration 10: Certificate from a copper plate engraved by Paul Revere, 1773 or earlier, containing blanks to be filled in by the Lodge. Used by St. Andrew's Lodge, 1774. Photographed with permission of the Grand Lodge of Masons in Massachusetts, A.F. & A.M.

XII

PAUL REVERE—MASONIC DECLINE

After 1800, Paul Revere turned his attention towards his business ventures. In that year he made his move from North Square to the brick house on Charter Street. He was also still the "enterprising mechanic" who operated a foundry at No. 13 Lynn Street, where he cast ironware, cannon, bells, copper bolts and spikes. As a mason, it seems that Revere held no masonic offices after 1800, and only occasionally attended meetings. In March 1801, while Revere was still working on the "Golden Urn," he purchased an old powder mill on the east branch of the Neponsett River in Canton, Massachusetts, which he intended to convert into a copper-rolling mill. By October 1801, Revere had rolled his first sheet copper, the first ever produced in the United States. Along with other government commissions, Revere provided the copper sheeting for the new State House dome in 1802. He is mentioned infrequently in the Grand Lodge minutes for 1802 and 1803, probably due to the amount of time he spent at Canton. By 1804, he wrote that "I have spent the last three years most of my time in the country, where I have mills for Rolling sheets and bolts, making spikes and every kind of copper fastenning for ships." Revere mentioned that his son and business partner, Joseph Warren, "takes care of the business in Boston," probably meaning the bell foundry, while "I take care at Canton about 16 miles from Boston."[118]

Despite his business commitments, Revere was present at a Grand Lodge meeting on June 11, 1804, when he was added to a committee concerned with "the number and grades of Lodges under this Jurisdiction." In September 1804, he was also involved with a committee raised to ascertain the charter dates. In October 1805, Paul Revere again served as a pallbearer, this time at the masonic funeral of Past Grand Master John Cutler, Esq. Cutler had been one of the pallbearers, along with Paul Revere, who had marched in the funeral procession of George Washington. Revere and the pall-bearers were directed to "dress in black and wear cocked hats, white scarves with black knots . . . and new white gloves and plain aprons." On October 9, 1804, a gale destroyed the roof of Revere's Boston foundry and the bell-making operations were moved to Canton. Although his business, named Paul Revere and Son, was now located entirely in Canton, Revere owned the house on Charter Street until his death, spending summers at "Canton Dale" and winters in Boston. Even if Paul Revere's participation in masonic activity diminished after 1800, he still continued to house the white marble urn at Charter Street until at least 1809. By this time, events were occurring which brought Rising States Lodge to the attention of the Massachusetts Grand Lodge. Since Revere's participation in the Grand Lodge was sporadic at best after 1800, it is likely that he also diminished or entirely ceased his activities with Rising States Lodge. Although minutes do not exist to support this, events would suggest that Revere had little active involvement with Rising States Lodge by 1809.[119]

XIII

EXIT RISING STATES LODGE

After 1800, Rising States Lodge continued its association with the Massachusetts Grand Lodge, regularly paying dues and sending representatives to Lodge meetings. In 1804, the rank of Rising States Lodge was secured by a Grand Lodge committee appointed to "ascertain the dates of the Charters of the several Lodges." The committee concluded that rank and seniority must be determined from the date of the charter. Paul Revere was on this committee, which decided that

> Rising States Lodge, being formerly St. Andrews and so received under the jurisdiction of the Grand Lodge, by mutual agreement, on the express condition of enjoying the rank of St. Andrews Lodge, does, of right rank with the date of the original charter of said Lodge.

The rank of Rising States Lodge remained unchallenged until late 1809, when St. Andrew's Lodge was finally admitted under the jurisdiction of the Massachusetts Grand Lodge. Although for many years St. Andrew's Lodge had chosen to remain under the Grand Lodge of Scotland, it was permitted to take rank in the Massachusetts Grand Lodge "at all their Quarterly Communications, Festivals and Funerals, and all other regular and constitutional meetings" from the date of its charter, November 30, 1756, placing it directly below St. John's Lodge in rank. This was the position which Rising States Lodge had formerly enjoyed.[120]

The masons of Rising States Lodge, perceiving a "competition of rank" between themselves and St. Andrew's Lodge, submitted a complaint to the Grand Lodge in March of 1810. A committee of five was chosen to confer with Rising States Lodge, which held several "free conferences" over the next several months. By June 1810, upon reviewing the original complaint, the committee concluded that the facts proclaimed by Rising States Lodge were "correctly and truly stated," but they were also "of opinion that others do exist which are not there stated, which would have a material influence on the Grand Lodge in deciding on the subject." It seems that the Grand Lodge committee perceived problems in Rising States Lodge which ran deeper than a discontent over rank. In December 1810, nearly one year after the issue of rank arose, a committee from Rising States Lodge took their seats at a meeting of the Grand Lodge. It was doubtful whether they had a right to vote, since Rising States Lodge "had determined on an early resignation of their Charter to the Parent Grand Lodge." This committee also confirmed that "a dissolution had taken place as a Lodge and a division of their funds contemplated." Rising States Lodge then surrendered its records, and their Master resigned the charter. The Grand Lodge immediately raised a committee "after some debate" to investigate the "propriety of accepting the resignation of their Charter." The dissolution of a Lodge was hardly a common occurrence, and it remained the task of this committee to investigate the causes of Rising States Lodge's dissolution and suggest a course of action. Although the committee was directed to report at the next meeting, nine months elapsed before they finally made their report.[121]

In September 1811, the committee investigating the conduct of Rising States Lodge described an undesirable situation marked by "discord and uneasiness." They observed a steady decrease in Lodge funds, which stock, when sold, amounted to $1,527.50. This sum "together with the proceeds of the regalia, furniture, etc. of the Lodge was divided among the nominal members thereof." A majority of members voted "Yea" upon the question of dissolving the Lodge, including Paul Revere, Jr. and Amos Lincoln. Once the vote to dissolve was carried, it was suggested that "when the charter shall be returned to the Grand Lodge, it be accompanied by all the stock, jewels, regalia, etc; the stock to be under the direction of the Grand Lodge for charitable purposes." The majority of Rising States Lodge voted against this "important question," with only five members voting in the affirmative. It also appeared that several of the masons who voted upon these questions were not even official members of Rising States Lodge according to the last return of officers, yet they were considered members and received a dividend during the division of funds. Paul Revere was among these several brethren. Paul Revere, Paul Revere, Jr. and Amos Lincoln all received a dividend of the Lodge stock. In order to further investigate "the causes which led to the late unhappy occurences," the Grand Lodge committee summoned the twenty members of Rising States Lodge to appear before them at Masons' Hall in April 1811. Thirteen of the twenty, including Paul Revere, Jr. and Amos Lincoln, answered the summons.[122]

The problems of Rising States Lodge were apparent from the members' testimonies. The committee was "perfectly satisfied" that "discord and uneasiness" had plagued the Lodge "for five years past," long before the question of rank arose in 1809. Although Rising States Lodge did take offense to the admission and rank of St. Andrew's Lodge, its discontent was seen as the result of "old animosities and internal dissentions" since every Lodge, not only Rising States, had been superceded in rank by the addition of St. Andrew's. During the committee's investigation, several members of Rising States Lodge reported "increasing difficulties." Some attributed these difficulties to "the dissapointment of certain characters in not being elected to the first offices of the Lodge." Others blamed the appointment of the Grand Lecturer. Whatever the cause, the committee described a situation where

> members were generally at variance with each other; that great opposition was made to the admission of candidates, in consequence of which there was an accession of very few members; and that applications for charity, even from members, were seldom attended to, and when relief was granted to a distressed Brother, it was with a sparing hand . . .

The committee was "irresistably compelled" to conclude that a "spirit of disorganization" had prevailed in the Lodge for many years before the "now pretended cause of the dissolution." They viewed "with the most serious apprehension the conduct of the late Rising States Lodge" which they saw as "an alarming precedent, tending to excite a spirit of disorganization, inducing lodges to take offense on the slightest occasion, that they might have a plausible pretext to obtain possession of the funds."[123]

The committee reminded Rising States Lodge of the proper usage of masonic funds. The charity fund, enlarged through initiatory fees and member generosity, was clearly intended "for the relief of the unfortunate," this being "the principal advantage derived to society from the Masonic Institution." If the funds were made an "object of speculation" or if they were used for "the purposes of festivity or the aggrandizement of the Lodge," this would destroy the ancient landmarks of masonry and encourage dissolution, not to mention the poor example given to future generations and potential donors. The committee finally declared that "assuming the right to divide these funds is an alarming and dangerous innovation and must essentially undermine the foundation of the Institution which every member is obliged to support." The Grand Lodge feared that it might be necessary "to adopt measures to prevent Lodges accumulating property which may excite into action the rapacious desires of designing and unprincipled men." The conduct of the Lodge was clearly inexcusable.[124]

According to the Grand Lodge committee, the most alarming aspect of the misconduct was that the actions of Rising States Lodge appeared to be "countenanced and supported by men of respectable and influential standing in Society, whom we have been in the habit of esteeming, and who have held high and responsible stations in the Masonic family." This would certainly have included Paul Revere.

Revere did receive a dividend of the Lodge stock although he was no longer officially a Lodge member. Paul Revere may have shared the opinion of John Tuckerman, who was serving as Junior Warden during the dissolution. Tuckerman claimed that "great disunion" prevailed in the Lodge where "applications for charity were seldom allowed" and where there existed a "general disposition not to admit new members." Tuckerman decided that since "such was the state of the Lodge," it would be for "the best interests of masonry" if the Lodge was dissolved. It was only to bring about the dissolution that he agreed to serve as Junior Warden. Possibly due to the testimony of masons such as Tuckerman, the Grand Lodge committee took a different view of the dissolution, realizing that "the late members of Rising States Lodge were actuated by very different motives in voting for a dissolution and disunion which took place; some to put a stop to the waste and disorder which had become apparent and thereby secure the remnant of the funds for charitable objects."[125]

If this were true, the Grand Lodge was willing to let the members of Rising States Lodge express the "purity of their principles and the sincerity of their actions." In the spirit of masonic reconciliation, the Grand Lodge asked each member of Rising States Lodge who had received a dividend to come forward and give evidence that their share of the stock had been used for charitable purposes. By June 1812, the committee had served three separate notices upon the members of Rising States Lodge calling for their testimonies. Paul Revere was among those who appeared before the committee. He claimed that "the money rec'd by him, as his proportion of the stock, had been all faithfully applied to the relief of the distressed members of the Masonic family." As of December 1812, masons who failed to answer the summons were "expelled from the Institution of Masonry."[126]

XIV

PAUL REVERE—MASONIC BUSINESSMAN

Paul Revere's involvement with Freemasonry was negligible after the dissolution of Rising States Lodge in 1812. This was not an abrupt change for Revere, as his active involvement had been decreasing steadily since 1800, probably due to his new business in Canton, Massachusetts. It is ironic that Revere's business commitments contributed to the decrease of his masonic activity, since there had always existed a happy union between business and masonry throughout his life. William Bentley, who purchased a bell from Revere in 1801, was only one of many masonic acquaintances who brought their business to Revere. Paul Revere himself also mixed masonry and business. In 1808, he wrote to the Reverend George Richards in Portsmouth, New Hampshire, congratulating him on his masonic discourse, of which Revere had received a copy and read "with a great deal of pleasure." Revere felt that "every mason who reads it must acknowledge, that the precepts, and Sentiments it contains, bespeaks the Mason, the Christian, and the Man." After wishing good health to the Reverend and his family, Revere closed the letter with a postscript from Paul Revere & Son. After first apologizing for mentioning the matter, Revere explained that he had delivered a bell to the Reverend's church in December 1807, the debt being $379.68. Since his letters had gone unanswered and he did not know "who are the ostensible persons to write to," Revere asked the Reverend if he would "enquire into the matter and write us." Although Paul Revere's later businesses enjoyed the patronage of masonic customers to some extent, the relationship between masonry and business was most clearly pronounced during Revere's period as a goldsmith.[127]

Paul Revere was first introduced to the goldsmith's art by his father, a French Huguenot emigré who came to Massachusetts in 1715 and apprenticed with Boston goldsmith John Coney. Paul Revere in turn apprenticed in his father's shop and became its chief craftsman after his father's death in 1754. He was then nineteen years old. After serving two years as a soldier during the French and Indian War, Revere was settled in Boston again by 1756. At the age of twenty-five, in 1760, Paul Revere received the first masonic degree in St. Andrew's Lodge. Masonic customers swiftly followed. Lodges were in need of many items which a goldsmith could produce, such as jewels, seals, ladles and medals. A goldsmith who also did engraving could provide necessary plates for certificates and summonses. Paul Revere made all of these things, and more. His Wastebooks reveal that he did not leave his masonic connections in the Lodge room.[128]

Paul Revere's goldsmith shop was located at the head of Clark's wharf, the second busiest wharf in Boston. It was a good location, providing access to the maritime trade and those who worked in connection with it. It is not surprising that Paul Revere numbered several ship captains among his customers. Before the American Revolution, business was good and Revere made silver for many prominent Bostonians, although these were not the majority of his customers. Revere probably inherited his father's clientele, and he interacted with all classes of people, making silver and gold items for friends, neighbors and relatives, among others. After 1760, Revere could include fellow masonic brethren among his list of social acquaintances and customers. When Revere began keeping accounts in 1761, his first recorded order was for a masonic item. In 1761 and 1762, he made "Masons Medals" for three masons, all from his own Lodge. It was a pattern which would continue throughout his days as a goldsmith. (See Appendix 5.)[129]

An examination of Paul Revere's Wastebooks for the goldsmith shop reveals that he benefited financially as well as socially from his masonic connections. Revere's goldsmith period lasted from approximately 1756 to 1799, overlapping with several other businesses that he created and nearly coinciding with his years as an active mason. While many of his customers appear only once, others regularly brought business to Revere, and provided a base of loyal support for his other business ventures. A significant number of Paul Revere's customers were masons, and it is likely that they patronized him specifically because he was a mason. A sampling of 309 customers from the years 1761 to 1796 reveals that approximately 146 were fellow masons. Unfortunately, there are no figures recording the total number of masons in Massachusetts during Paul Revere's goldsmith period. It has been estimated that, in 1776, there were only 100 lodges with no more than 5,000 masons in all of the thirteen colonies combined. Considering these figures, it is likely that only a small fraction of Boston's 16,000 people in 1775 were masons. If the masons in Massachusetts were only a small percentage of the population, it is all the more significant, and hardly coincidental, that nearly one-half of Paul Revere's customers were masons.[130]

Paul Revere was a logical choice for masonic patronage. Not only was he a fine craftsman, but his association with the masons assured his fellow brethren that he was a man of high principles. He also had the unique knowledge of the Craft which enabled him to produce items of symbolic masonic significance, unlike most Boston goldsmiths of his day. Revere received his first masonic order in 1761, not five months after his initiation, and produced his last, the golden urn, forty years later. In the intervening years, he took at least twenty-four orders for masonic items that he recorded in his Wastebooks, and he produced no fewer than forty items altogether.[131]

It was no coincidence that Paul Revere's first three masonic orders involved masons from St. Andrew's Lodge, as he frequently did work for masons and Lodges known to him personally. Revere's masonic orders represent at least twenty different Lodges, no fewer than six of which were in Boston. Revere was personally involved with three of these—St. Andrew's Lodge, Rising States and the Massachusetts Grand Lodge—the others were St. John's, the Massachusetts Lodge and Columbian Lodge. Several orders came from traveling Army Lodges such as Washington Lodge No. 10 and the American Union Lodge. Revere could also include among his customers several of the Lodges which he chartered while Grand Master, as he made officers' jewels for Bristol, St. Paul's and Washington Lodges. (See Appendix 4.) He also made several items for Tyrian Lodge of Gloucester, which he was active in founding. In 1770, Tyrian Lodge voted Revere thanks "for the zeal and activity he has shown and extended in the establishment of this Lodge." He also served as its proxy for several years. The majority of Revere's masonic orders came from Lodges in Massachusetts, from as far as Nantucket, Newburyport and Marblehead, or as near as King Solomon's Lodge across the river in Charlestown. Revere also had business dealings with three Lodges in Maine and one in Surinam (Dutch Guiana). Despite the distance of these Lodges, the representatives of each were all masons who had been previously associated with St. Andrew's Lodge, where they would have had the opportunity for personal contact with Paul Revere.[132]

Not only did Paul Revere, as a working goldsmith, serve a wide variety of Lodges, but he also produced a varied assortment of masonic items. Many of his orders were for "jewels," the symbolic emblems of Lodge officers. Revere made no fewer than eleven sets of officers' jewels, containing anywhere from five to twelve jewels (see Illustration 9), although a number was not usually specified in his Wastebooks. He did not always make complete sets of jewels. For John Jenks, he made "a Masons jewel," while for Tyrian Lodge he crafted "two Stewards Jewils." The jewels were usually of silver. Several other items which he made for masonic customers suggest officers' jewels, such as the pairs of "Cross Keys" made for both Simon Greenleaf and the Tyrian Lodge, and the "p Silver Cross pens" crafted for Samuel W. Hunt. The crossed keys usually signified the Lodge Treasurer, while the crossed pens represented the Lodge Secretary. A set of jewels in 1782 earned Revere £11.12.0. One year later he charged

£9 for five masons' jewels, and in 1795, he received £8.12.6 for a set of nine jewels. Four additional Lodges paid Revere £12 for jewel sets in the years 1784 and 1797.[133]

Other masonic items made by Paul Revere include medals, seals, punch ladles and copper plate engravings. Revere began copper plate engraving as early as 1764, producing trade cards, cartoons, portraits and magazine illustrations, among other things. Copper plate engraving was a logical extension of Revere's work as a goldsmith, which often involved the engraving of skillful designs and family arms upon pieces of silver. As early as March 1762, he received an order for a "Copper Plate for Notifications," which suggests a masonic use. Lodges regularly issued notifications or summonses to their members, informing them of the time, dates and locations of meetings. Lodges also used certificates and diplomas, which were awarded to masons as they advanced through the three degrees. Revere made at least six notifications for specific Lodges, as well as several certificates. At least two of his certificates were engraved for general use, with blanks to be filled in with the name of the Lodge, the recipient, the degree and the date. (See Illustration 10.) Before Revere began making masonic engravings, the diplomas and notices were made out by hand (and continued to be in some cases). Revere generally copied his designs from English masonic sources.[134]

While some masons engaged Paul Revere specifically to make jewels, notifications, seals and medals, the majority of Revere's masonic customers did not order masonic items, but rather patronized Revere for the large variety of silver and gold items which he produced and sold. Even James Graham, who probably entered Revere's shop in January 1761 to buy himself a "Free Mason Medal" also purchased a "Pair of Silver Knee Buckles." Simon Greenleaf, a mason from Newburyport, purchased a "Frame and Glass for a picture" and a "Floor Cloth" along with a masonic "plate for Notifications" in September 1772. Edward Foster and Captain Winthrop Sargent, both masons, purchased silver punch ladles from Revere in 1763 and 1783 respectively. It is not known whether these ladles were used for masonic Lodges. The same holds true for a "silver medal" purchased in 1789 by Moses M. Hayes, who was then Grand Master. Samuel Barrett purchased two ladles from Revere in 1762 and donated them to St. Andrew's Lodge, but most of the masons who came to Revere's shop made purchases which were entirely unrelated to their masonic Lodges.[135]

It is not known what Paul Revere's early goldsmith shop looked like, but it must have contained a workshop, as well as an interesting assortment of finished and unfinished products. Although Revere made most pieces to order, he also sold many smaller ready-made items, such as silver shoe and knee buckles, and buttons of gold and silver. While he periodically received large orders from wealthy patrons, most of Revere's work involved single pieces of silver. He made teaspoons, ladles, creampots, tankards, sugar dishes, pepper casters, canns, porringers, teapots, coffee urns, butter boats and sugar tongs, among other things. In gold, he made rings, bracelets and necklaces, as well as the occasional turtle shell rings and buttons. A list of "stock ready made in the cases" from September 1783 indicates the variety of small, commonplace items which Revere sold in his shop. The stock included buckles of all types, spoons, buttons, hairpins, brooches, soup and punch ladles, and gold rings and necklaces. While he only stocked one gold ring and necklace, he had numerous quantities on hand of other items, such as thirteen hairpins, forty-three brooches, twelve salt spoons and many buckles. He also had ready-made two cream pots, sugar tongs, and several unusual buttons, such as "3 pr Mocoa Stone Butt^n sett in gold." He would also have carried his blank masonic certificates for ready sale.[136]

Revere enjoyed the patronage of fellow Freemasons throughout his goldsmith years, despite the disruption caused by the Revolutionary War. Until the American Revolution, Paul Revere operated his business from the shop on Clark's Wharf, although in 1770 he had moved his residence to a house in North Square. The outbreak of hostilities disrupted Revere's business completely, as it did the functioning of the masonic community. According to his Wastebooks, Revere's business had been steady up until April 1775, with the exception of a sharp decrease in entries for the year 1770. The last entry was recorded April 1, 1775, with the next not being entered until December 19, 1778. Afterwards, the few scattered entries had little to do with the goldsmith shop. It was not until 1780 that business began to proceed normally, suggesting that Revere abandoned his goldsmith trade for five years while concentrating on the war-related activities. During that time, he made his famous ride to Lexington, and did not return to Boston until the British left in March of 1776. By April 10, 1776, Revere received his commission as a major in the regiment raised for Boston's defense. By fall, he was a lieutenant colonel commanding at Castle Island in Boston Harbor, which further removed him from his work. Due to the disruption of masonic meetings during this period, it is unlikely that there was any great demand for masonic items, although if Revere produced any, he made no record of it.[137]

In 1780, Paul Revere resumed his goldsmith business with an eye towards the future. By 1782, he wrote to his French cousin that "I now follow my business again of a Goldsmith + trade a little." The trade became more important as the war drew to a close. When the peace treaty ending the War of Independence was signed in September 1783, Paul Revere was prepared to receive a shipload of imported wares from England, which had been unavailable during the war years. He had already opened "a large store of hardware" for these goods before September 1783. The store was located opposite Liberty pole, where the famous Liberty tree had once stood. It included his goldsmith shop. An inventory from February 1785 reveals the assortment of merchandise that Revere stocked. Along with various "plated ware," such as candlesticks, coffee urns, goblets, cream pots and other items, he sold pewter, brass and copperwares, cutlery, door locks, nails, looking glasses, spectacles, buttons and buckles, japanware, tinware, writing paper, razors and scissors, wallpaper, combs, fabric, and tools. Despite Revere's debut as a merchant, he still continued to function as a goldsmith. In 1786, when he moved his store to 50 Cornhill, near the market at Dock-Square, he assured his customers that "the Goldsmiths Business is there carried on in all its Branches; all kinds of Plate made in the newest taste, and finished in the neatest manner." The hardware store attracted many of the same people who patronized Paul Revere as a goldsmith, including masons. One ledger from the hardware store for the years 1783 to 1788 contained an alphabetized index of seventy-nine customers. Of the seventy-two complete names listed, nearly one-half were masons.[138]

Just as masons patronized Paul Revere's business ventures, Revere also sought out fellow masons for needed goods and services. Samuel Danforth, who was initiated into St. Andrew's Lodge in 1764, was Paul Revere's doctor. In 1783, Revere paid him for medicine and attendance to his family for the years 1770 through 1783. When Revere needed work done on a house owned by his aunt, Mrs. Mary Marett, in 1768, he turned to "Bouve & Stodder," two masons from St. Andrew's Lodge. Gibbons Bouve was a housewright who became a mason in 1765, while Asa Stodder, a bricklayer, was initiated in 1764. At a cost of £6.11.6, they supplied "85 feet of Bord & Planck" and "Sundry Nails" with which they performed "Sundry Job *Don* to the house." In 1776, Revere again hired Bouve to build a small barn on his North Square property. Bouve charged Revere £3 for "Building your Cow House" and £2.16.8 for "350 feet of Board."[139]

Paul Revere owned his North Square house for thirty years, from 1770 until 1800. Although he lived at the house through most of the Revolutionary period, his residence was sporadic after 1780, when he began renting the building. At least two of his tenants were fellow masons. On May 27, 1780, Revere wrote that he "lett my House at the North End to Mr George D^{e}france for twenty five Spanish mill Dollars P Quarter, or as much paper as will purchase them at the time the Rent is due." This was probably the same George DeFrance who served as an officer of Friendship Lodge in 1780, and was cleared of charges brought against him in September 1781. He was still paying rent to Revere in August of 1781. By 1784, Revere was again renting his house to a mason. On April 19, Joseph Dunkerley leased the house for £45 per year, where he conducted "his Profession of Painting in Miniature." Dunkerley was still residing there in 1786. He had become a member of St. Andrew's Lodge in July of 1776, and was also active with Paul Revere in Rising States Lodge.[140]

XV

CONCLUSION

Despite his lifetime of service to the masonic fraternity, it is still a topic of speculation why Paul Revere chose to become a mason. Numerous reasons, both abstract and concrete, can be cited which may help to explain Paul Revere's masonic involvement. If nothing else, masonry provided a source of recreation and social activity. Lodge meetings brought men together on at least one evening each month for discussion and refreshment, enabling them to participate in an exclusive fraternity characterized by distinctive language, rituals and badges, all of which its members evidently enjoyed. Although most masons took the purpose of the society seriously, it was also a social club, and the friendships begun there were often extended into other areas of life. In this way, Paul Revere enjoyed financial support from fellow masons who patronized his goldsmith shop, his hardware store and his foundry. Although Paul Revere must have been aware, as a young goldsmith, that he would derive long term financial benefit from masonic affiliation, it is unlikely that this was his only motive for becoming a mason.

Although it is difficult to offer a comprehensive description of the typical mason during the Revolutionary period, it is likely that Paul Revere and others recognized the society as a potential avenue of opportunity. While Lodges in the early Republic attracted a diverse membership from varying occupations and income levels, several studies indicate that masons tended to be mobile, politically active men who often held positions of leadership in their communities. Masonry likewise offered Paul Revere an opportunity to exercise and sharpen his leadership abilities, which he used significantly in Revolutionary activities, particularly among his fellow artisans. Throughout Revere's life, masonry offered the most constant means by which he displayed his leadership potential, since, unlike other patriot leaders, he held few public offices. It is also possible that, in joining a Lodge, Paul Revere hoped to associate with influential men who might not otherwise have been included within his immediate social circle. Although Revere's own Lodge primarily contained artisans like himself, masons frequently met fellow brethren from other

Lodges. Through masonic affiliation, Paul Revere gained an instant relationship with men of like thought and character, useful in both his business and social life.[141]

A powerful attraction of Freemasonry was also the ideology itself. The society emphasized a respect for tradition, enforcing the belief that men could create a better world through reason, harmony and right conduct. Masonry fit well with prevailing Protestant virtues, yet represented the liberal religious attitudes of the day. Being a secret society with an exclusive membership, masonry appealed to men as a group set apart, entrusted with a unique purpose and driven by the highest ideals. For Paul Revere, masonry probably broadened his thinking as well as his circle of acquaintances, and the fraternity may have been instrumental, with its liberal Enlightenment tendencies, in smoothing the way in men's minds toward political revolution. Although there were masons who remained loyal to England, the fraternity did place Paul Revere in close contact with radical thinkers like Joseph Warren, who undoubtedly influenced Revere, exposing him to men and ideas that he might not otherwise have known intimately.

After nearly fifty years as a mason, Paul Revere ended his masonic association as inexplicably as he had started it, leaving behind no record of why he left the fraternity. The little he actually wrote about Freemasonry—his Cornerstone Speech, his Ceremony for Constituting a New Lodge and his farewell address—all reveal a sensitivity and affection for the Craft. He must have enjoyed the pomp and ceremony of the aged traditions, particularly when he filled the Chair of Solomon as Grand Master from 1795–1797. In 1796, fellow mason William Bentley noted simply that "Col. Revere enters into the Spirit of it, and enjoys it." Revere again entered "into the Spirit of it" twenty-one years later in 1817 when he wrote to Grand Master Francis Oliver that

> On examineing some old papers, a few days since, I found The inclosed paper, the writing, and signature of which, I know to be the hand writing of Joseph Warren Esq, late Grand Master, who lost his life on Bunker's hill in the year 1775. From the manner and cause of his Death, there can be but few copies of his hand writing to be found. For the perusal of the Craft, and for the information of all men I wish you to have this paper enroled among the Archives of the Grand Lodge. Boston, Septem^r 1, 1817

Paul Revere's letter to the Grand Lodge came after years of inactivity, and less than one year later, on May 10, 1818, he died. No masonic mourning greeted Paul Revere's death. Revere does not seem to have had a masonic funeral and his will did not specify that he receive one. He could only hope that the Grand Lodge would preserve his memory, as he encouraged that they remember Joseph Warren.[142]

Paul Revere's contribution to the Craft was worth remembering. He was an early initiate in the first Ancient Lodge in Boston, and spent at least fifty of his eighty-three years as an active mason. He was involved in creating the Massachusetts Grand Lodge of Ancient Masons, through which he participated in the organization and spread of masonry throughout the State. By the time he was Grand Master, the Grand Lodge of Massachusetts was chartering Lodges in Massachusetts, Maine, Vermont, Connecticut and New Hampshire. Paul Revere also played a role in writing the final resolution which declared the independence of the Grand Lodge—well in keeping with his desire for an independent America. He saw Massachusetts Freemasonry through the hazardous transition from colony to state, and experienced the brunt of the turmoil through St. Andrew's Lodge. He created a new Lodge which eventually failed, and perhaps disillusioned him, but he offered the Craft his loyalty, and constantly worked through offices and committees to preserve and perpetuate its integrity. His was the glorious age of masonry, prior to the antimasonic crusade of the 1820s, when the Society grew unhindered and flourished in public processions and ceremonies, laid cornerstones and attracted men of influence in every community. Paul Revere was not the least of many distinguished men who served the fraternity and enjoyed its benefits.

In simple terms, Paul Revere expressed his feelings about the fraternity during his farewell speech in 1797. He assured his brethren that the society was devoted to high ideals, and he encouraged them to remember that "the Cause we are engaged in is the Cause of Humanity, of Masons and of Man." Paul Revere was an ordinary man who lived a life of extraordinary service and accomplishments. His masonic association can only serve to reinforce the impression of his patriotism and integrity which endures in the popular imagination.[143]

NOTES

[1] For a sketch of the origins of American Freemasonry, see Earl W. Taylor, *Historical Sketch of the Grand Lodge of Masons in Massachusetts From Its Beginnings in 1733 To The Present Time* (Boston, Massachusetts: Grand Lodge of Masons in Massachusetts, 1973), pp. 3–4. See also Louis C. King, "The Grand Lodge of Massachusetts Birthplace of Freemasonry," *Trowel* 1 (April 1983): 6. Paul Revere's birthdate is difficult to determine precisely. For Revere's birth, see Esther Forbes, *Paul Revere and the World He Lived In* (Boston: Houghton Mifflin and Company, 1942), pp. 16, 453 and Elbridge Henry Goss, *The Life of Colonel Paul Revere*, 2 vols. (Boston: Joseph George Cupples, 1891), 1: 10–11. Goss noted information from the *New England Historical and Genealogical Register*, vol. 19, p. 235 (no date given), which published the records of the New Brick Church for 1722–1775. This church was located in Boston's North End on present-day Hanover Street and was attended by Revere's parents. According to these records, Paul Revere was baptized on 22 December 1734. Goss claims that Revere was born 21 December, the previous day. Taking into consideration the change in the calendar being used during this period, Goss records the date of birth as 21 December 1734, O.S. (old style) and 1 January 1735, N.S.(new style). Ten days are added to old style dates in the winter. Since the church records listed Revere's baptism only, it is not clear to this writer how Goss determined the exact date of birth. Forbes also takes into account the calendar change. She does not mention Revere's actual birthdate, but places his baptism on 22 December 1734, O.S. and 1 January 1735, N.S. The membership files at the Grand Lodge of Massachusetts A.F. & A.M., Boston, Massachusetts, list Revere's birth as 21 December 1734. While this may be information supplied by Revere himself, researchers should be aware that the Lodge membership files have largely been reconstructed, due to the loss of many early records through fire.

[2] On St. Andrew's Lodge founding see Taylor, pp. 6–7 and King, p. 6. For a "Table of Lodges Chartered by Massachusetts Grand Lodges from 1733–1792" see Grand Lodge of Masons in Massachusetts, *Two Hundred And Fifty Years of Massachusetts Masonry* (Boston: Rapid Service Press, 1983), pp. 16–17, hereafter cited as *Two Hundred and Fifty Years*. For a history of St. Andrew's Lodge see *The Constitutions of the Ancient and Honorable Fraternity of Free and Accepted Masons: Containing their History, Charges, Addresses and Collected and Digested from Their Old Records, Faithful Traditions and Lodge Books. For The Use of Masons To Which are added The History of Masonry in the Commonwealth of Massachusetts, and the Constitution, Laws and Regulations of Their Grand Lodge together with a Large Collection of Songs, Epilogues, etc.* (Worcester, Massachusetts: published by the Massachusetts Grand Lodge, printed by Isaiah Thomas, 1792), p. 134. This refers to Section II, which deals with the History of St. Andrew's. This source hereafter cited as *Constitutions*. See also *Centennial Memorial of the Lodge of St. Andrew* (Boston: Printed by vote of the Lodge of St. Andrew, 1870),

p. 160. Reference to the founding of St. Andrew's Lodge can be located in the section entitled "Reminiscences of the Green Dragon Tavern," pp. 160–73. Information from this section will hereafter be cited as "Reminiscences". This volume was compiled for a centennial celebration and contains many sections which deal with various subjects. Several significant sections will be cited by name throughout these notes. On Ancient vs. Modern controversy see Mervyn Jones, "Freemasonry," in *Secret Societies,* ed. Norman MacKenzie (New York: Crescent Books, Inc. 1967), pp. 162–63. It is Jones who attributes the Ancient/Modern split to disagreements over ritual, dating from the *Book of Constitutions* of 1722-1723. He makes no mention of a class distinction in the split. King, p.6 explains the formation of St. Andrew's Lodge along class lines. He attributes the Ancient split in England to a clash between Irish workmen and the gentlemen's lodges in London, claiming that similar class conflict may have caused the formation of St. Andrew's Lodge. This may be true, since St. Andrew's was composed mainly of artisans, while St. John's membership was reportedly more "elite". Even if this theory were true, this writer would hesitate to attribute this as the only reason for the founding of St. Andrew's Lodge. Taylor, pp. 6–7, suggests that St. Andrew's Lodge was formed in response to the Ancient/Modern rift in England.

[3] For a definition of eighteenth century Freemasonry see *Constitutions,* p. 18. Also see the page entitled "Sanction" at the front of the volume for Revere's involvement. On medieval history of masonry and levels of masons see Jones, pp. 158–59, 161. See also Harry Carr, *Six Hundred Years of Craft Ritual* (Grand Lodge of Missouri, 1977), pp. 1–4.

[4] On the history of masonry, see Jones, pp. 161–62. For reference to guilds, social clubs and lodges see Dorothy Ann Lipson, *Freemasonry in Federalist Connecticut, 1789–1832* (Princeton: Princeton University Press, 1977), pp. 5–6, 15, 19–22. Although she deals with Connecticut, Lipson begins her book with a chapter on "The Invention of Freemasonry," which traces the origins of the fraternity in England and describes the type of men who formulated modern Freemasonry.

[5] These ideas are condensed from Lipson's chapter on "The Invention of Freemasonry." See especially pp. 6–7, 13–30, 37–39.

[6] On speculative and operative masons, see *Constitutions,* pp. 17–18 for quotes. On history of masonry, see Jones, pp. 161–62. It is Jones who says that masonry was in full flower by 1735. Carr, p. 1. claims that the ritual was virtually standardized by 1813. According to William Preston Vaughn, *The Anti-Masonic Party in the United States 1826–1843* (Lexington, Kentucky: The University of Kentucky Press, 1983), p. 10, the transition from operative to speculative masonry lasted nearly two hundred years. He also adds that the distinction was still being made between operative and speculative masons in London, 1720. For founding of the Grand Lodge of England, see *Two Hundred and Fifty Years,* p. 1 and Lipson, pp. 23–33.

[7] See Allen E. Roberts, *The Craft and Its Symbols: Opening the Door to Masonic Symbolism* (Richmond, Virginia: Macoy Publishing and Masonic Supply Company, Inc., 1974), pp. 25, 35–36, for references to King Solomon's Temple and St. John's Feasts. According to Roberts, the first reference to St. John the Evangelist as a mason's patron appeared in 1598. See Elmer T. Kemper, "Hiram, King of Tyre 'Pillar of Strength'," *California Freemason,* Summer 1973, p. 112 for Solomon's Temple. According to masonic tradition, Hiram assisted Solomon in building the temple and was originally the Grand Master of all Freemasons until he yielded his preeminence to Solomon. See Hannah Mather Crocker, *A Series of Letters on Freemasonry by a Lady of Boston* (Boston: Printed by John Eliot, 1815), p. 17 for a discussion of masonry and religion, including quote on Jesus. The letters were written between Crocker and a

young potential mason seeking information about the society. They were signed "A. P. Americana" and "Enquirer", appearing in the *Centinel* in 1810. The author (1765–1847) was a daughter of Reverend Samuel Mather and granddaughter of Cotton Mather. See Forbes, pp. 164–167 for a description of Crocker's view of her native North Square. See *Constitutions*, pp. 17–18, 165, 175 for all other quotes on religion and references to pillars. This volume contains a brief section "Concerning God and Religion." See Jones, pp. 159, 162 for references to Solomon's Temple and religion. See Lipson, pp. 18–19, 37–38 for role of the church and a discussion of Freemasonry as the "Universal Religion."

[8] On quotes about eternal laws and masonic moral system see John Ward Gurley, *An Address on the Origin and Principles of Freemasonry* (Boston: Printed by Brothers Russell and Cutler for St. John's Lodge, 1800), p. 18. See *Constitutions*, pp. 19, 172 for quotes on "ignorance, superstition, etc . . ." and the "benign influence of masonry." See Lodge of St. Andrew Minutes of Lodge Meetings, Microfilm 1778–1854, Grand Lodge of Massachusetts A.F. & A.M., Library, Boston, Massachusetts for quotes on atrocious crimes (2 May 1780) and attempts to discredit masonry (25 March 1784). This source hereafter cited as "St. Andrew's Lodge Minutes." For a general explanation of Freemasonry see Kathleen Smith Kutolowski, "Freemasonry and Community in the Early Republic: The Case for Antimasonic Anxieties," *American Quarterly* 34 (Winter 1982): 545–49.

[9] See *Constitutions*, pp. 19, 172 for quotes on moral system and brotherly love. See also Crocker, p. 10. See Gurley, p. 17 for quote on masonry as a "fabric". For masonic qualities see Thaddeus Mason Harris, *Masonic Emblems Explained* (Boston: Printed by William Spotswood for the subscribers, July 1796), pp. 10, 11, 14, 18–19. In 1792, Thaddeus Mason Harris was "Librarian of the University of Cambridge" and was appointed by the committee compiling the masonic volume of Constitutions to "regulate and superintend the publication of said book." See "Sanction," *Constitutions*. See *Proceedings of the Most Worshipful Grand Lodge of Ancient Free and Accepted Masons of the Commonwealth of Massachusetts In Union with the Most Ancient and Honorable Grand Lodge in Europe and America, According to the Old Constitutions. 1792–1815* (Cambridge: Press of Caustic—Claflin Company, 1905) p. 81 for reference to the masonic funeral of 14 December 1795. This volume of proceedings hereafter cited as *Proceedings* Vol. 2.

[10] See *Constitutions*, p. 176 for the first quotes here concerning benevolence and charity in the section "A Charge at Initiation into the First Degree." Also find quote about "relief to fellow creatures" in this section. See also Crocker, p. 7. See Harris, p. 20 for a "liberal bestowment of alms." See Gurley, p. 14 for the statement that "the obligations we are under, compel us in the exercise of charity to make a discrimination in favor of the members of our fraternity . . . from amoung our neighbors, friends, and our relatives." See *Centennial Memorial*, p. 111 for reference to Boston Overseers of the Poor. With regards to money, currency and its value varied widely throughout the American colonies and states prior to 1792, when the dollar was established on the decimal system as the monetary unit for the United States. Even after 1792, the use of the British pound still persisted in monetary transactions for several decades. For a detailed discussion of colonial money and its value see John J. McCusker, *Money and Exchange in Europe and America, 1600–1775—A Handbook* (Chapel Hill: The University of North Carolina Press, 1978). See *Proceedings* Vol. 2, p. 496 for quote on the "principal advantage . . ." This statement was made by a Grand Lodge Committee on 9 September 1811 while investigating a possible misuse of funds occurring in Rising States Lodge. Revere was a founder of this Lodge and it will be dealt with later in this work.

[11] See St. Andrew's Lodge Minutes, 9 September and 14 October 1779 for charity donations; April 1783 for Phillip Bass petition and 13 March 1783 for Pulsifer petition. See *Proceedings* Vol. 2, pp. 496, 465–66 for references to initiation fees, quarterages and charity fund. Several early references exist in St. Andrew's Lodge Minutes to charity regulations and a charity fund. Despite this mention of a fund, many charity requests involve "passing the hat" for money, with very few references to the Lodge "stock." Consequently, it is difficult to know how much money the charity fund contained and how it was used. The *Proceedings* Vol. 2, pp. 465–66 (30 January 1811) discusses the establishment of a charity fund, although it is difficult to believe that the Grand Lodge did not have a Charity Fund until 1811.

[12] See *Constitutions*, p. 172 for section on "Behavior towards a Strange Brother." See St. Andrew's Lodge Minutes, 12 November 1778 and 10 September 1783 for quotes.

[13] See *Constitutions*, p. 166 for quote on "persons admitted members of a Lodge . ." in Section III "Of Lodges." See also p. 178 for quote on acquaintances. For information about admitting candidates see "Charter and By Laws of the Lodge of St. Andrew held in Boston, New-England Constituted in the year 1756," Items 16–20, Lodge of St. Andrew, Charters and Bylaws, Microfilm 1760–1778, 1855–1872, Grand Lodge of Massachusetts A.F. & A.M., Library, Boston, Massachusetts. This reel contains nothing but charters and bylaws, beginning with the first (1756) and recording every change even into the nineteenth century. The charter quoted here is the first one on the reel. This source will be hereafter cited as "St. Andrew's Lodge Charters."

[14] See St. Andrew's Lodge Charters 1756, Item 24 in the Bylaws for punishment for disclosing Lodge transactions. For two quotes, see *Constitutions*, p. 171, under sections "Behaviour in Presence of Strangers not Masons" and "Behaviour at Home and in Your Neighborhood."

[15] See St. Andrew's Lodge Charters 1756, Items 8, 14, 15, 23 and 26 in the Bylaws. See St. Andrew's Lodge Minutes, 13 February 1766 for reference to "stamping with the foot." In the actual minutes, the word appears to read "striking" although it is not clearly written. In the *Centennial Memorial*, p. 270 (13 February 1766), the word is printed as "stamping". See St. Andrew's Lodge Minutes, 11 May 1769 for Huzza reference; 9 March 1780 for account of Captain Allen, and 14 December 1780 for Robert Fairservice. See *Constitutions*, p. 170 for warning against excessive behavior in section "Behavior after the Lodge is over and the Brethren not gone." For quote of young potential mason see Crocker, pp. 11–13.

[16] Crocker, pp. 13–14. For information on Tavern, refreshment and feast days (24 June 1772, 27 December 1773) see "Reminiscences," *Centennial Memorial*, pp. 161, 164–65. Liquor was not permitted during Lodge meetings. According to St. Andrew's Lodge Charters, 11 February 1773, "It is recommended to the Master not to allow any liquor on the table until the business of the Lodge is over." For an earlier reference to liquor see Lodge of St. Andrew, Minutes of Masters' Lodge Meetings, 24 May 1764, Microfilm 1762–1802, Grand Lodge of Massachusetts A.F. & A.M., Library, Boston, Massachusetts. In the Masters' Lodge, it was even "voted that as soon as the Lodge is closed the closets be closed and no liquor be brought out after." Paul Revere was a member of the Masters' Lodge, which held meetings separate from the regular Lodge. This source hereafter cited as "St. Andrew's Masters' Lodge." For reference to purchase of food by committees see St. Andrew's Lodge Minutes, 31 August and 11 October 1781. See also 30 November 1768 for smoking and 24 June 1772. For reference to smoking see *Centennial Memorial*, p. 271, on 30 November 1768, when it was "voted that there shall be no smoking when the Lodge is open, only when called to refreshment." For

references to Stewards see pp. 269, 271. These references in the *Centennial Memorial* are in a section entitled "Chronology," pp. 265–290, which is a chronological history of the Lodge of St. Andrew from its founding to 1870. This section will hereafter be cited as "Chronology."

[17] For quotes see Crocker, p. 7. See St. Andrew's Lodge Charters 1756, Items 1 and 3 in the Bylaws for times and days of St. Andrew's Lodge meetings. See St. Andrew's Masters' Lodge Minutes for meeting times. For meeting days of the Massachusetts Grand Lodge see *Proceedings in Masonry. St. John's Grand Lodge 1733–1792: Massachusetts Grand Lodge 1769–1792* (Boston: Published by the Grand Lodge of Massachusetts, Press of Rockwell and Churchill, 1895), pp. 226–27 (12 January 1770). This source is hereafter cited as *Proceedings* Vol. 1.

[18] See *Commemoration of the One Hundred and Fiftieth Anniversary of the Lodge of St. Andrew 1756–1906* (Boston: Printed by vote of the Lodge of St. Andrews by The Riverside Press, Cambridge, Massachusetts, 1907), p. 294. See pp. 273–301 for a listing of "Initiates and Members." This source is hereafter cited as *Commemoration of Lodge of St. Andrew*. According to a file card on Revere at the Massachusetts Grand Lodge Library, it is not certain on what day Revere actually earned the second degree. Minutes show that the second degree was conferred on several candidates on 8 January 1761, and Paul Revere was present, so that he could have been "passed" on this date. For quote about merit see *Constitutions*, p. 167. For quote beginning "in due time . ." see St. Andrew's Lodge Charters 1756, Item 21 in the Bylaws. For initiation of Revere see *Centennial Memorial*, p. 96. See Roberts, *The Craft and Its Symbols*, for a good explanation of the symbolism, moral rhetoric and ceremonies involved with earning the three degrees.

[19] See Forbes, p. 58 for Revere's possible impression of St. John's Lodge, and pp. 42–46 for military experiences. For references to Gridley's Lodge see *Two Hundred and Fifty Years*, pp. 16–17; Henry J. Parker, *Army Lodges During The Revolution* (Boston, 1884).

[20] See *Centennial Memorial*, pp. 241–42 for "A List of Members of the Lodge of St. Andrew, With Their Occupations and Residences, Made at Communications Held in Royal Exchange Tavern, King Street, Boston, The 2d Thursday of January, 1762." This source hereafter cited as "List of Members." This list is reproduced as Appendix 1. See Forbes, p. 99 for comment on "elite" membership of St. John's Lodge.

[21] For reference to Revere's initiation, see Goss, 2:465–66. It is Goss who claims that the charter was received on the same day that Revere was initiated. Goss footnotes this to the *Centennial Memorial*, 1870, without noting a page number. The actual minutes of St. Andrew's Lodge do not mention the charter on 4 September 1760. The only reference to Paul Revere reads "Paul Revere made an Entered prentiss." See King, p. 6 for mention of the charter and Revere's initiation. See *Commemoration of Lodge of St. Andrew*, pp. 284, 285 for initiation dates of Nathaniel and Robert Hichborn. See *Centennial Memorial*, p. 268 for initiation of Joseph Warren. According to the St. Andrew's Lodge Minutes, Warren was originally initiated on 30 September 1761, being "proposed to be raised to Master" on 28 January 1762. He attended few meetings and on 14 November 1765, he was "readmitted a Member of the Lodge," after which time he was an active member. According to "Chronology," *Centennial Memorial*, p. 268, Warren was entered as an Entered Apprentice on 10 September 1761 (note discrepancy with the Lodge minutes) and passed to Fellow Craft on 2 November 1761.

[22] For use of Tavern see "Reminiscences," *Centennial Memorial*, pp. 160, 167–69. For St. Andrew's meeting places see "Chronology," *Centennial Memorial*, pp. 267–68. See St. Andrew's Lodge Minutes, 12 January 1764 for quote on

buying a house. See St. Andrew's Masters' Lodge 1762–1764, for several references to meetings held at "Brother Stones." It is not clear whether Stone owned a business, or if the meetings were at his home.

[23] Roberts, p. 12 claims that the interlaced square and compass was the symbol of Freemasonry from at least the beginning of the eighteenth century. See *Centennial Memorial*, pp. 179, 181 for physical description and purchase of the Tavern in "Speech of Dr. N. B. Shurtleff." The Tavern was demolished October 1828 for the widening of Green Dragon Lane. See "Chronology," *Centennial Memorial*, p. 269 for name change. See also "Reminiscences," *Centennial Memorial*, pp. 160–161 for Green Dragon Tavern name changes, and p. 164 for text of the public announcement of 20 December 1773. See St. Andrew's Lodge Minutes, 18 February 1768 for the only mention in the minutes of "Catherine Ker." See 14 June 1764 for the meeting held "at Freemasons Hall which this evening was Named by a vote of the Lodge." There were no references in St. Andrew's Lodge Minutes to the Tavern being called "Freemasons Arms," although in the Grand Lodge *Proceedings* Vol. 1, frequent references are made to meeting at Masons' Arms, Free Masons' Arms, or Masons' Arms Tavern, even after the name was changed to Masons' Hall. Spelling and punctuation in eighteenth century records are rarely consistent, and the name also appeared frequently in the singular without an apostrophe. When an apostrophe was included, it was actually placed before the 's' of masons. For examples of how the Tavern name appeared, see *Proceedings* Vol. 1, p. 235 (1 March 1771); p. 243 (4 December 1772); p. 246 (12 December 1772); p. 282 (2 June 1780) and p. 287 (12 January 1781).

[24] See St. Andrew's Lodge Minutes, 18 February 1768 for account of Tavern purchase and eight purchasers. See 13 April and 10 May 1764 for first Lodge meetings. See 12 October 1764 for Thomas Crafts. See "Chronology," *Centennial Memorial*, p. 270 for references to rebuilding the stable and Milliken's bill. It is not recorded who billed the Lodge for the stable work. Although these two items were included in the "Chronology," this writer did not see them in the St. Andrew's Lodge Minutes. See *Centennial Memorial*, p. 181 for the first Lodge meeting. See "List of Members . . ." *Centennial Memorial*, pp. 241–42 for masons' occupations. (See Appendix 1.) According to Shurtleff, Thomas Milliken was a victualler by occupation, who was Chairman of the Committee to buy the House. Shurtleff wondered if Milliken might have been landlord of the Tavern at some time. However, the 1762 List of Members shows him to be a Bricklayer.

[25] See St. Andrew's Lodge Minutes, 10 May 1764 and 14 February 1765 for references to Committees dealing with the House. See 30 November 1763 for election of Burbeck. See also 12 October 1764, 9 and 10 July 1767.

[26] St. Andrew's Lodge Minutes, 11 and 18 February 1768, 10 March 1768.

[27] St. Andrew's Lodge Minutes, 10 March 1768, 11 April 1771, 9 July 1772, 22 April and 13 May 1773. The Dispensation which allowed St. Andrew's Lodge to continue functioning was probably not obtained from Scotland, due to the short period of time indicated, but from the Massachusetts Grand Lodge, a Grand Lodge of Ancient Masons formed in Boston in 1769. Its formation is discussed in a later section of this work. According to the *Proceedings* Vol. 1, p. 247 (7 May 1773), St. Andrew's Lodge presented a petition to the Grand Lodge claiming that "they had been deprived of their Charter of Erection by Mr. Will[m] Burbeck (a former Master of said Lodge). Praying a dispensation may be Granted them from this Grand Lodge, untill they can obtain a Coppy of their Charter from the Grand Lodge of Scotland . . ." The minutes of St. Andrew's Lodge provide no details as to why Burbeck was retaining the Charter and whether it had anything to do with his acquiring the Tavern for the Lodge.

[28] St. Andrew's Lodge Minutes, 10 February 1774. See 13 December 1776 and 24 January 1777 for evidence of Burbeck's good favor. The Lodge voted to reconsider his suspension of 1773, and he presented a Book of Constitutions to the Lodge. See 15 December 1777 for the final vote in the House matter.

[29] St. Andrew's Lodge Minutes, 10 March 1768, 12 May 1768, 14 July 1768, 11 August 1768, 13 October 1768, 8 October 1772, 10 June 1773.

[30] See "Chronology," *Centennial Memorial,* p. 271 for quotes on Standing Committee, raising rents, and regimental music. For reference to regiments see p. 272 (14 December 1769). See p. 276 (2 May 1780) for "Rent of Green Dragon £ 40 hard money." See St. Andrew's Lodge Minutes, 12 June 1767 for reference to rent; 30 November 1768, 12 January 1769, 11 May 1769 and 14 December 1769 for Lodge dealings with soldiers; 2 May 1780 and 22 March 1781 for raising rents; 4 December 1782 for Massachusetts Charitable Society, and 12 December 1781 for Perfect Union Lodge. See Forbes, pp. 133, 139–40 for Paul Revere quote and reference to soldiers.

[31] For reference to a box for the charter and jewels, see "Chronology," *Centennial Memorial,* p. 268 (10 July 1760). See St. Andrew's Lodge Minutes, 10 July 1760, 4 September 1760, 18 December 1760, 12 February 1761, 12 March 1761, 30 November 1762. For references to ladles see Waste and Memoranda Book for the workshop at Boston, 19 November 1762, Revere Family Papers, Microfilm Roll 5, Volume 1, Massachusetts Historical Society, Boston, Massachusetts. Paul Revere produced two surviving volumes of accounts for his goldsmith shop. They cover the period 1761–1783 and 1783–1797, and can be found on Microfilm Roll 5, Volumes 1 and 2, respectively. Since the Historical Society refers to these volumes as "Wastebooks," they will hereafter be cited as "Paul Revere, Wastebooks."

[32] See St. Andrew's Lodge Minutes, 14 May 1761 for vote on feast, and 30 November 1762.

[33] See St. Andrew's Lodge Charters for regulations and bylaws of the Lodge. See St. Andrew's Masters' Lodge 10 September 1762, for meetings of the Masters' Lodge beginning in September 1762. Before 1762, Masters' Lodge minutes are included with the regular St. Andrew's Lodge minutes. It is likely that in Revere's day, the early Boston Lodges granted only the first and second degrees, while the third degree was conferred in the Masters' Lodge, which was a separate institution. See St. Andrew's Lodge Minutes, 27 January 1761.

[34] For raising of fees, see St. Andrew's Lodge Minutes, 30 November 1762, 12 and 26 March 1778. Other references to fees in the early minutes are 1 December 1766, 8 November 1770, 2 December 1771, 10 October 1776, 3 June 1777 and 15 December 1777. Instances of the rapid conferment of degrees appear frequently in the Lodge minutes, three such examples being 13 May 1762, 15 November 1769, and 14 February 1771. At this last meeting, "Brother Wells being bound to Sea soon—was Passed as a Fellow Craft and afterward had the Sublime degree of a Master Mason Confer'd on him by a Unan. Vote," all during the same evening.

[35] See St. Andrew's Lodge Charters 1756 for list of officers and descriptions of duties. See *Constitutions,* p. 167 for quote about Master and further information about officers in the section "of Masters, Wardens, Fellows and Apprentices." The description of officers given here is compiled from both of these sources, for both the Grand Lodge and St. Andrew's Lodge, although there is some discrepancy in the description of duties. The tasks of some officers are not fully described in either source. The jewels described are analogous to those pictured in Illustration 3. The symbols of the jewels are relatively standard. See Roberts for a discussion of masonic symbolism, which also touches upon the symbolism of the jewels.

[36] For Paul Revere's offices see Appendix 2 of this work. According to the St. Andrew's Lodge Minutes, the Lodge almost always met more than once a month, usually in Lodges called for "special occasion." The following is a list of the number of meetings held by St. Andrew's Lodge from 1760 to 1777: September–December 1760—9; 1761—26; 1762—19; 1763—18; 1764—15; 1765—12; 1766—16; 1767—16; 1768—19; 1769—18; 1770—13; 1771—13; 1772—15; 1773—18; 1774—15; January—April 1775—4; April—December 1776—10; 1777—48.

[37] See Appendix 2 for Paul Revere's masonic offices. The St. Andrew's Lodge Minutes list the presiding officers at every meeting. In 1762, Revere served as Junior Warden on 11 February, 8 April and 13 May. He served as Senior Warden on 28 January, 29 April and 29 July. In 1764, he served as Senior Warden on 9 February, 13 April, 10 May and 26 June. In 1765, he served as Lodge Master on 9 May, 10 October and 14 November. He served as Senior Warden on 10 February 1763, and as Junior Warden on 12 June 1766. In 1767, he served as Junior Warden on 10 April, as Senior Warden on 12 June and 10 September, and as Secretary on 9 October and 30 November.

[38] See St. Andrew's Lodge Minutes for frequency of Revere's attendance. For committees dealing with Revere and feast day celebrations see 16 June 1762, 9 June 1763, 13 December 1764, 11 December 1766. The feast days were for St. John the Baptist on June 24 and St. John the Evangelist on December 27. For funeral committees and Revere, see 9 June 1768, 13 April 1769, 11 May 1769 and 8 June 1769. A committee raised on 9 January 1766 to form regulations may also have dealt with funerals, although the writing is illegible. Revere was on this committee. For charity committees in 1766, see 13(?) February, 10 April and 14 August. See 1 December 1766 for John Rowe subscription. For other examples of Lodge charity see 12 February and 11 April 1761, 8 April and 9 September 1762, 13 April, 12 May, 11 July, and 13 October 1763, 29 December 1766, 8 January 1767, 13 July and 12 November 1769, 11 July and 13 December 1770. Paul Revere also served on several additional committees between 1760 and 1770. See 10 May 1764 for committee about Green Dragon Tavern. See 9 January 1766 and 8 December 1768 for committees writing to Scotland. Also see 9 July 1767 and 9 August 1770.

[39] See "Reminiscences," *Centennial Memorial*, p. 166 for brief history of Royal Arch Chapter. It finally united with another chapter and became the Royal Arch Chapter of Massachusetts in 1798. See Jesse Ames to Librarian, 5 May 1953, Paul Revere file, Grand Lodge of Massachusetts A.F. & A.M., Library, Boston, Massachusetts for a letter about the acceptance of Revere and Joseph Warren in the Chapter, including quote on Revere. See also *Celebration of the One-Hundred and Twenty-Fifth Anniversary of St. Andrews Royal Arch Chapter 1769–1894* (Boston: Published by the Chapter, Printers S.J. Parkhill and Company, 1894), pp. 46–47, 10–11.

[40] See *Constitutions*, p. 134, section on History of St. Andrew's Lodge for quote about "jurisdiction infringed . . ." For quote beginning "outlawry . . ." and for responses of St. Andrew's Lodge, see "Chronology," *Centennial Memorial*, pp. 268–271 (17 February 1761, 8 April 1761 1 February 1763, 30 November 1765). See also St. Andrew's Lodge Minutes, 12 February 1761. The reference to writing Scotland in 1763 appeared in the "Chronology" of the *Centennial Memorial*. This writer did not find reference to it in the St. Andrew's Lodge Minutes. The "Chronology" also included a reference in November 1765 to a "vote of retaliation" passed by St. Andrew's Lodge "not to admit members of any of the Lodges of the town as visitors" until St. John's lifted its similar ban against St. Andrew's. This writer did not see any reference to this in the St. Andrew's Lodge Minutes for November 1765, although a similar vote was passed by St. Andrew's in November 1767. See J. Hugo Tatsch, *Freemasonry in the Thirteen Colonies* (New York: Macoy Publishing and Masonic Supply Com-

pany, 1929), pp. 33–34 for account of hostilities. For detailed account of controversy see *Centennial Memorial*, pp. 22–31, a section by Charles W. Moore entitled "Address: The Massachusetts Grand Lodge and its Relations With St. Andrew's Lodge," given 23 December 1869.

[41] See St. Andrew's Lodge Minutes, 22 January and 6 February 1766 for quotes about a "happy coalition" and the "ill Grounded" response of St. John's Lodge; 12 June and 10 July 1766 for reference to letters written to Scotland; 30 November 1767 for vote of St. Andrew's Lodge. Although the Lodge minutes mention the address given to St. John's and the reply of that Lodge, the text of these documents is not included with the Lodge minutes. The quote about "harmony and sincere friendship . . ." and those dealing with the "offensive votes" of St. John's Lodge were found in the *Centennial Memorial*, pp. 22–31, in the address delivered by Charles W. Moore in 1869. His address included quotations from original sources. See also Tatsch, pp. 33–34.

[42] See "Chronology," *Centennial Memorial*, pp. 271, 272 (30 November 1768, 30 May 1769, September 1769). See also St. Andrew's Lodge Minutes, 30 November and 8 December 1768, 14 December 1769. See *Centennial Memorial*, pp. 194–95, and 31–32 for Warren's appointment and extent of jurisdiction. See *Proceedings* Vol. 1, pp. 456–57, for text of document from 3 March 1772 which extended Warren's authority, making him "Provincial Grand Master over all the Lodges on the Continent of North America, which now are or hereafter shall be Erected and taken to hold of the Grand Lodge of Scotland . . ." The British military Lodges were No. 106 Registry of Scotland, the Duke of York's Lodge from the Sixty-fourth Regiment, the Lodge No. 58 Registry of England from the Fourteenth Regiment, and Lodge No. 322 Registry of Ireland with the Twenty-ninth Regiment. See Appendix 2 for Paul Revere's offices in the new Grand Lodge.

[43] See *Centennial Memorial*, pp. 32–33 for military Lodges and list of officers of the Grand Lodge. See "Chronology," *Centennial Memorial*, pp. 272, 273 (19 September 1769 and 12 December 1771) for St. Andrew's Lodge references. See also St. Andrew's Lodge Minutes, 19 September 1769, 12 December 1771. See Appendix 5 of this study for goldsmith work done by Paul Revere for masonic use. See *Proceedings* Vol. 1, pp. 226–27 (12 January 1770) and pp. 232–33 (14 October 1770, 7 December 1770, 6 December 1771).

[44] See *Two Hundred and Fifty Years*, p. 20 for date of Tyrian Lodge. See *Proceedings* Vol. 1, p. 231 (14 October 1770) for quote on Tyrian Lodge and p. 232 (7 December 1770) for Revere as Master of St. Andrew's Lodge when "Br Paul Revere presented from St. Andrew's Lodge the following List of Officers . . ." For mention of Revere's elections as Senior Grand Deacon see pp. 226–27 (27 December 1769); p. 232 (7 December 1770); p. 234 (1 March 1771); p. 237 (6 December 1771); pp. 243–44 (4 December 1772) and p. 251 (3 December 1773). According to the records of Tyrian Lodge, Paul Revere was involved with the Lodge from its founding. On 24 April 1770, "it was voted that the thanks of the Tyrian Lodge be returned to Bro. Paul Revere for the zeal and activity he has shown and exerted in the establishment of this Lodge, and at the same meeting it was voted that Bro. Paul Revere represent us in the Grand Lodge at the Ensuing Quarterly Communication. This he has continued to do, acting as our proxy for several years." He resigned as Proxy when he was elected Master of St. Andrew's Lodge in 1777. This information was included in Earle J. T. Merchant, Secy., Tyrian Lodge to Librarian, Grand Lodge of Massachusetts, 22 April 1967, in the folder "Paul Revere Project," Grand Lodge of Massachusetts A.F. & A.M., Library, Boston, Massachusetts.

[45] See *Two Hundred and Fifty Years*, pp. 18, 19 for Massachusetts and Tyrian Lodges. See *Proceedings* Vol. 1, pp. 230–31 (10 August 1770) for Lodge installa-

tion. See p. 231 (14 October 1770), p. 233 (7 December 1770) and p. 236 (6 December 1771) for Lodge dues. See pp. 237–38 (6 March 1772) about Newburyport Lodge and p. 240 (6 November 1772) for Portsmouth quote. The Grand Lodge *Proceedings* list Revere as Master of Tyrian Lodge, which is incorrect, since he served only as proxy.

[46] See Appendix 2 for Revere's offices. See *Proceedings* Vol. 1 for Revere's attendance and number of meetings. See p. 244 for Revere election in 1772 (4 December 1772) and p. 255 (7 September 1774) for Revere as Treasurer.

[47] See *Proceedings* Vol. 1, pp. 238–43 for account of the 24 June 1772 feast. For preparation and follow-up committees, see pp. 238–39 (29 May 1772) about music and p. 243 (4 September 1772).

[48] See *Proceedings* Vol. 1 for account of feasts, pp. 262–63, 267–70 (4 December 1777, 4, 18 and 28 December 1778).

[49] *Constitutions*, p. 170.

[50] See Forbes, pp. 117–19 for reference to Long Room Club. See *Proceedings* Vol. 1, pp. 245–46 (12 December 1772) for mention of Grand Lodge advertising Feast of St. John. For 29 November 1773 announcement see "Excerpts from Diary of John Rowe," *Proceedings* Vol. 1, p. 427. John Rowe was Grand Master of the Lodge of St. John.

[51] "Chronology," *Centennial Memorial*, p. 274 (30 November 1773). For account of tea party see "Reminiscences," *Centennial Memorial*, pp. 169–170. See *Proceedings*, Vol. 1, p. 428 for quotes on tea party and number of people present from John Rowe Diary Excerpts. See also St. Andrew's Lodge Minutes, 30 November 1773.

[52] For quotes from John Rowe see *Proceedings* Vol. 1, p. 428. See "Chronology," *Centennial Memorial*, p. 274 (16 December 1773). See also St. Andrew's Lodge Minutes, 16 December 1773. See "Reminiscences," *Centennial Memorial*, pp. 169–70 for song and participants. For Revere's quote about ride to New York see Paul Revere to Jeremy Belknap in Massachusetts Historical Society, *Paul Revere's Three Accounts of His Famous Ride* (Portland, Maine: Anthoesen Press, 1968), n.p.

[53] See David Ammerman, *In the Common Cause: American Response to the Coercive Acts of 1774* (New York: W. W. Norton and Company, Inc. 1974), pp. 5–12 for information on the Coercive Acts. See also *Proceedings* Vol. 1, pp. 254–55 (3 June 1774, 7 June 1774, 2 September 1774).

[54] For Revere quote on dispatches, see Paul Revere to Jeremy Belknap, *Three Accounts*. For Suffolk Resolves, see Ammerman, pp. 74, 75, 130, 131. Also see Forbes, p. 218. It is Forbes who attributes the Resolves to Warren. See St. Andrew's Lodge Minutes for Paul Revere's attendance. In late 1774, the only meeting he attended was the election of officers on 30 November 1774.

[55] For Revere quotes on watching soldiers see Paul Revere to Jeremy Belknap, *Three Accounts*. See *Proceedings* Vol. 1, p. 258 for "Memo 19 April 1775." See also St. Andrew's Lodge Minutes for lapse of meeting between April 1775 and April 1776.

[56] For use of Tavern as hospital see *Centennial Memorial*, p. 180 in a letter from Lieutenant-Governor Thomas Oliver to Rev'd Doc'r Caner, Col. Snelling, Maj. Paddock, Cap. Gore and Cap. Gay.

[57] See *Centennial Memorial*, pp. 111–112 for a description of St. Andrew's Lodge in the war years, including the references to thanks from Scotland, the Dutch Mason, and the 1777 collection for the poor. See "Chronology," *Centennial Memorial*, pp. 276–77 for references to the Dutch Mason, British prisoners of war and distressed brethren (12, 17 February 1778, 15 January 1779, 14 March 1782). See St. Andrew's Lodge Minutes, 12 and 17 February 1778, 15 January 1779, 14 March 1782.

[58] *Proceedings* Vol. 1, pp. 267, 269–70 (4, 28 December 1778); p. 275 (4 June

1779); pp. 286–87 (27 December 1780); p. 296 (21 December 1781); p. 300 (24 June 1782); p. 379 (24 June 1791).

[59] See Taylor, pp. 8–9 for Warren's death and crisis in the Lodge. For quote about the search for Warren's body, see *Constitutions*, pp. 137–38 (18 March 1776). For quote about the Grand Lodge not holding meetings during the British occupation, the *Constitutions* also records, under 19 April 1775, that "on this memorable era, hostilities commenced between Great Britain and America; immediately upon which the town of Boston became a garrison and was abandoned by many of its inhabitants, so that the regular meetings of the Grand Lodge were suspended." For the first meeting after the war started, see *Proceedings* Vol. 1, p. 258 (27 December 1776).

[60] See Forbes, pp. 124–25, 300, 302–303 for references to dentistry, Warren's burial, Revere and Morton. For quote see *Constitutions*, pp. 137–38 (18 March 1776). The *Constitutions* account records only that Warren was identified "by an artificial tooth," making no specific mention of Revere. Forbes attributes the identification to Revere. References to Revere's dental work also occur in "Paul Revere, Wastebooks," 1761–1797. One example, on 5 March 1774, records work done for John Joy, which Revere notes as "To Cleaning Your Teeth & one pot Dentfrice." The cost was four shillings and six pence.

[61] *Constitutions*, pp. 138–40 (27 December 1776, 8 March 1777). For quote beginning "to All Masters and Wardens . . ." concerning the summons and meeting, see *Proceedings* Vol. 1, p. 259 (14 February 1777) and p. 260 (8 March 1777). See also p. 462 for quote beginning "together with the Delegates . . ." This quote is from an announcement of Webb's election sent "To All the Fraternity of Ancient Free and Accepted Masons Around the Globe Greeting . . ." This is included in an appendix which contains pertinent masonic documents. Taylor, pp. 9–10 gives account of Webb's election. Paul Revere and Joseph Webb were again elected to the same offices in December 1778.

[62] All quotes are from an address delivered to the Grand Lodge by Josiah Bartlett on 24 June 1790. See *Proceedings* Vol. 1, pp. 370–73 (24 June 1790). See also pp. 301–303 (6 December 1782) for a report issued by the Grand Lodge which also justified the independent election of Webb.

[63] See Forbes, pp. 305–7 for Revere's position on Castle Island. For Revere's offices in the Grand Lodge see *Most Worshipful Grand Lodge of Ancient Free and Accepted Masons of the Commonwealth of Massachusetts Directory 1981*, pp. 108–110. Also see *Proceedings* Vol. 1, p. 261 (8 March 1777); pp. 262–63 (4 December 1777) and p. 267 (4 December 1778). See also Appendix 2 of this work. For Revere as Master of St. Andrew's Lodge see list of "Past Masters" in Lodge of St. Andrew November 1982 brochure. See also St. Andrew's Lodge Minutes, 2 December 1777. Also consult this source for Revere's attendance. For Craft's "musick" see *Proceedings* Vol. 1, pp. 262–63 (4 December 1777).

[64] See St. Andrew's Lodge Minutes, 11 February 1779 for Lottery; 9 September and 14 October 1779 for monetary gifts; 10 December 1778 for references to Moses Deshon, sconces, aprons, Lottery and Manasseh Marston and 15 January 1779 for quote on Marston negatives. All master masons were entitled to wear an apron, a symbolic article of clothing reminiscent of the aprons worn by working stone-masons. By the nineteenth century, they were often decorated with masonic symbols. For date of Manasseh Marston membership see *Commemoration of Lodge of St. Andrew*, p. 289 in list of "Initiates and Members." See Carol Ely, "North Square: A Boston Neighborhood in the Revolutionary Era," (Boston, March 1983), pp. 4–5, 38 for references to Manasseh Marston, who was a cooper. A copy of this paper can be found in the Paul Revere House Library.

[65] See Goss, 2: 326, 336–37, 387 for information on Penobscot Campaign. See also Forbes, pp. 340–47. See St. Andrew's Lodge Minutes, 30 November

1779 for election and guote. See Minutes also for Revere's attendance. See *Proceedings* Vol. 1, p. 267 (18 December 1778) for reference to Revere's military rank. For additional information on the Penobscot campaign see Matthew Cassidy and Linda Webster, "Paul Revere, An Officer and a Gentleman: The Penobscot Campaign of 1779," (Boston, 1983). A copy of this paper can be found in the Paul Revere House Library.

[66] St. Andrew's Lodge Minutes, 30 November 1779, 9 March 1780, 2 May 1780, 30 November 1780, 30 November 1781. See 12 December 1781 for Revere proposing masons.

[67] St. Andrew's Lodge Minutes, see 14 December 1780, 8 March 1781, 25 February 1782, 14 March 1782, 5 October 1782.

[68] St. Andrew's Lodge Minutes, 22 March 1781, 10 May 1781, 18 May 1781, 4 December 1782, 12 June 1783.

[69] For Revere offices, see *Proceedings* Vol. 1, p. 261 (8 March 1777); pp. 262–63 (4 December 1777); p. 267 (4 December 1778); p. 277 (3 December 1779); p. 285 (1 December 1780) and p. 297 (1 March 1782). For quote, see pp. 298–99 (10 June 1782). See pp. 301–303 (6 December 1782) for the complete text of the report signed by Revere and three other masons. The report is reprinted almost verbatim in *Constitutions*, pp. 143–46.

[70] All quoted sections are from the December 1782 report. For complete text see *Proceedings* Vol. 1, pp. 301–303 (6 December 1782). Most of this report is also incorporated into *Constitutions*, pp. 143–46.

[71] For text of report see *Proceedings* Vol. 1, pp. 301–303 (6 December 1782) and *Constitutions*, pp. 143–46. For other accounts of Grand Lodge independence, see Taylor, p. 10 and Tatsch, p. 36. Tatsch claims that Joseph Webb was Grand Master until 1782, at which time John Warren was elected. According to *Proceedings* Vol. 1, p. 301, Joseph Webb was still Master on December 6, 1782, so it was he who issued the report of that date.

[72] See St. Andrew's Lodge Minutes, 16 December 1782 for taking the vote, and 23 January 1783 for copy of letter to Grand Lodge and decision to wait until peace is settled. For account of same events see "Chronology," *Centennial Memorial*, p. 277 (6 December 1782, 16 December 1782, 29 January 1783). See *Proceedings* Vol. 1, pp. 304–05 for receipt of St. Andrew's Lodge letter (24 December 1782) and mention of letter to Scotland (3 January 1783); p. 312 (4 December 1783) and p. 317 (31 March 1784) for references to circular letter.

[73] St. Andrew's Lodge Minutes, 12 December 1783, 22 January 1784. For a list of Yea and Nay voters see *Centennial Memorial*, p. 244 "Record of A.D. 1784." See also Appendix 3 of this work. "Chronology," *Centennial Memorial*, p. 277 (22 January 1784). John Warren was elected Grand Master 7 March 1783, and was still Grand Master in January 1784, at the time that St. Andrew's Lodge took its vote. For Revere appointment as Deputy Grand Master, see *Proceedings* Vol. 1, pp. 310–311 (4 December 1783) and *Constitutions*, p. 146. See *Constitutions*, pp. 167–68 for quote about the office of Deputy Grand Master in Section "of Masters, Wardens, Fellows and Apprentices."

[74] See St. Andrew's Lodge Minutes, 5 February 1784 for quotes and 12 February 1784 for Revere's role at the next meeting. Also see "Chronology," *Centennial Memorial*, p. 278 (12 February 1784). See p. 244 of this source for a list of masons who voted with Revere. See Appendix 3 for the list of "yea" and "nay" votes in January 1784.

[75] St. Andrew's Lodge Minutes, 12 February 1784.

[76] See "Chronology," *Centennial Memorial*, p. 278 (16, 25 March 1784) for reference to dividing the St. Andrew's Lodge property. No further explanation of this offer is given, which is quoted in full as it appears. See *Constitutions*, p. 147 (4 March 1784) for account of St. Andrew's split with Grand Lodge and quote beginning "to retain their ancient charter . . ." See St. Andrew's

Lodge Minutes, "Special Occasion" 25 March 1784. By 25 March, the St. Andrew's Lodge Minutes record that "a paper signed by Paul Revere . . .being read—together with the answer it is voted that they should be filed among the Lodge papers." Unfortunately, the minutes do not include the content of Revere's "paper" or the answer, but the paper was probably the lawsuit, which was discussed at this meeting. See *Proceedings* Vol. 1, pp. 314–15 (4 March 1784) for quote about relationship being ". . .at an End."

[77] See St. Andrew's Lodge Minutes, 14 October 1784 for content of 7 October letter to Scotland. See 25 March 1784 for all other quotes. There is *no* mention of the Revere lawsuit between the first reference on 25 March and the report of its being settled on 14 October. The latter reference is quoted in full.

[78] For accounts of the founding of the new St. Andrew's Lodge—later called Rising States Lodge—see *Constitutions*, pp. 147–48 and *Two Hundred and Fifty Years*, p. 19. See also Taylor, pp. 11–12 and *Centennial Memorial*, pp. 40, 106. See also Rising States Lodge, Minutes of Lodge Meetings, 29 March 1784, Grand Lodge of Massachusetts A.F. & A.M., Archives, Boston, Massachusetts, hereafter cited as "Rising States Lodge Minutes." The Grand Lodge Archives has the original minutes of Rising States Lodge from 29 March 1784 to 28 February 1785. Also see Paul Revere Record Book, March 1784, Grand Lodge of Massachusetts A.F. & A.M., Archives, Boston, Massachusetts for items purchased for Rising States Lodge, hereafter cited as "Rising States Lodge Record Book." Although most of this record book is devoted to Revere's personal accounts, the first few pages were used by him for Rising States Lodge from March 1784 to April 1786. According to this Record Book and Lodge Minutes, it is clear that Revere was the first Treasurer, although both Tatsch, p. 37 and the *Centennial Memorial*, p. 40 refer to Revere as the first Master. See *Proceedings* Vol. 1, p. 315 (4 March 1784) for the Grand Lodge acknowledgement of the new St. Andrew's Lodge, when it was noted that the "Return from St. Andrews Lodge Holding under this Grand Lodge was received, Accepted and Approved of."

[79] Rising States Lodge Record Book, 1784. Revere's financial records end with 22 April 1786, when his balance of money paid was £53.7.0. while the opposite side of the ledger also read £53.7.0. See Rising States Lodge Minutes, 26 July and 27 September 1784 for Revere on committee, and 27 December 1784 for "Col. Marston's State Street." When Revere and his minority split from St. Andrew's Lodge, they no longer met at the Green Dragon Tavern, nor did the Massachusetts Grand Lodge. After 1784, the Grand Lodge usually held its meetings at the Bunch of Grapes Tavern on State Street.

[80] Rising States Lodge Minutes, 31 May 1784, 25 October 1784, 28 February 1785. See Rising States Lodge Record Book, 25 April 1785, for reference to Charlestown Convention. For information and quote on convention see *Constitutions*, pp. 148–49 (3 March 1785, 26 May 1785).

[81] Rising States Lodge Minutes, 26 July 1784, 30 August 1784, 27 September 1784, 25 October 1784. For reference to name change and rank see *Two Hundred and Fifty Years*, p. 19 and *Centennial Memorial*, pp. 40, 106. For quote beginning "hold rank as . . ." see *Constitutions*, pp. 147–48. See also *Proceedings* Vol. 1, pp. 319–20 (2 September 1784) for quote about Charter and name change, and p. 356 (6 March 1789) for new Charter and rank. See Taylor, pp. 11–12 for confusion over name. The sources do not agree on the actual founding date of Rising States Lodge, a discrepancy existing between September 2 and 4, 1784. In Revere's Record Book, his accounts under the name of Rising States Lodge do not start until January 1785.

[82] See Rising States Lodge Minutes, 28 June 1784, 27 September 1784, 29 November 1784, 27 December 1784, 28 February 1785, for Revere's positions and "making" of Paul Revere, Jr. Since there are no minutes for Rising States

Lodge after February 1785, information about Revere's offices after 1785 has been gathered from the *Proceedings*. See *Proceedings* Vol. 1, pp. 322, 460 for Revere as Master at Bunch of Grapes meeting; pp. 324–25 for election on 2 June 1785 as Treasurer; pp. 359–60 (30 March 1789) for office in 1789, and p. 378 (2 June 1791) for 1791 election. See *Proceedings* Vol. 2, p. 29 (10 December 1792) for 1792 election. See Forbes, p. 190 for reference to Amos Lincoln. For Revere's offices in 1787–88, see "Rising States Lodge Return of Officers," 1787-5-28 and 1788-5-26, Grand Lodge of Massachusetts, A.F. & A.M., Archives, Boston, Massachusetts. For these two years, Amos Lincoln served as Senior Deacon (1787) and Junior Warden (1788).

[83] See *Proceedings* Vol. 1, pp. 359–60 (30 March 1789) for an account of the Grand Lodge visitation to Rising States Lodge.

[84] See *Proceedings* Vol. 1, for Paul Revere's attendance. For Revere's offices 1782–1792 see p. 297 (1 March 1782); p. 304 (6 December 1782); p. 311 (4 December 1783); p. 367 (3 June 1790?); p. 369 (24 June 1790) and p. 379 (24 June 1791). The Lodge held approximately eighty meetings between 1782–1792, of which Revere attended sixty-four. See *Proceedings* Vol. 1, p. 325 (2 June 1785); p. 343 (1 June 1787); p. 363 (4 June 1789); p. 368 (3 June 1790) for Revere and Lodge accounts.

[85] See *Proceedings* Vol. 1, p. 308 (5 September 1783) and pp. 309–310 (3 October 1783) for reference to rules and regulations. For references to Revere and Constitutions see p. 312 (4 December 1783) and pp. 335–36 (First Friday September 1786). A committee was also raised on 3 November 1786, p. 337, which did not include Revere. For long quote about printing constitutions, see p. 363 (4 June 1789).

[86] See Appendix 2 and note 84 for Paul Revere's offices. See *Proceedings* Vol. 1, p. 290 (22 May 1781) and pp. 293–94 (8 November 1781) for quotes on Lodges in Connecticut and Vermont. See also p. 321 (19 January 1785) for North Star; p. 316 (5 March 1784) for Keen, N. H. and p. 353 (18 December 1788).

[87] See *Proceedings* Vol. 1, pp. 359–60 (9 March 1789) for visit to Rising States Lodge; pp. 355-56 (6 March 1789) for Essex Lodge; p. 362 (4 June 1789) for Amity Lodge; p. 364 (3 September, 4 December 1789) for Wooster Lodge, and pp. 337–38 (3 November 1786) for quote "a Lodge at Danbury . . ." See *Proceedings* Vol. 2, pp. 41–42 (10 and 11 June 1793) for Lancaster and Worcester. See *Two Hundred and Fifty Years*, p. 18 for charter date and location of Wooster Lodge.

[88] See *Proceedings* Vol. 1, p. 280 (25 January 1780) for constituting Friendship Lodge; p. 284 (1 September 1780) for charges against DeFrance; pp. 287–88 (12 January 1781) for charges against Duplassius; p. 293 (7 September 1781) for quote about Revere and charges against Jareau; p. 365 (4 March 1790) and pp. 366–67 (2 April 1790) for Jutau case and quotes. See *Two Hundred and Fifty Years*, pp. 18–19 for charter dates of Friendship and Perfect Union Lodges.

[89] See *Proceedings* Vol. 1, pp. 287–88 (12 January 1781) for Bayley case, and p. 293 (7 September 1781) for decision on DeFrance. See Forbes, p. 346 for DeFrance renting from Revere. See also "Paul Revere, Wastebooks," 27 May 1780 for mention of rent.

[90] See *Proceedings*. Vol. 1, p. 288 (12 January 1781); p. 291 (1 June 1781); pp. 320–21 (2 December 1784). Due to his frequent committee work, it is clear that Revere was concerned with the behavior of Lodges and individuals. He wrote very little about Freemasonry, but the little he wrote does reflect these concerns. Revere deliberately mentioned that "Every free & accepted Mason ought to be sensible that subordination among Masons is as essential as in any Government whatever, & that without it no Society will flourish." He also recommended that the Lodges "be not suffered to break thro, or, treat with neglect any of the regulations of the Grand Lodge." See Paul Revere, "Address

to the Grand Lodge by R. W. Paul Revere, Esq. at the Meeting on the Evening of 11 December 1797," Grand Lodge of Massachusetts, A.F. & A.M., Archives, Boston, Massachusetts, hereafter cited as Paul Revere, "Address to the Grand Lodge."

[91] See *Proceedings* Vol. 1, p. 329 (8 December 1785); p. 337 (First Friday September 1786); pp. 344-45 (7 September 1787); pp. 347-48 (7 March 1788). The G:S probably stands for Grand Secretary.

[92] *Proceedings* Vol. 1, p. 351 (5 September 1788); pp. 374-75 (8 December 1790).

[93] See *Proceedings* Vol. 1, p. 286 (1 December 1780); pp. 295-96 (21 December 1781); pp. 297-98 (7 June 1782); p. 307 (6 June 1783); pp. 310-11 (4 December 1783); p. 325 (2 June 1785); p. 331 (8 December 1785); p. 334 (2 June 1786); p. 340 (1 December 1786).

[94] For reference to Revere's work with feasts from 1789-1792 see *Proceedings* Vol. 1, p. 362 (4 June 1789); p. 369 (10 and 24 June 1790), and pp. 377-79 (2 and 24 June 1791). For elections as an officer, see p. 278 (3 December 1779); p. 285 (1 December 1780); p. 297 (1 March 1782); p. 301-304 (6 December 1782); p. 310 (4 December 1783); p. 325 (24 June 1785), and pp. 367-68 (3 June 1790). Paul Revere was not present at this 1790 meeting, and the only office not listed is that of Deputy Grand Master. Since Revere appears as Deputy Grand Master at every other meeting in 1790, it is likely that he was finally chosen for the office. He was re-elected in 1791. See pp. 377-79 (2 and 24 June 1791). For Revere's offices in Rising States Lodge, see note 82.

[95] See *Proceedings* Vol. 1, pp. 316-17 (31 March 1784) for quote beginning "that a committee . . ." References to the Bunch of Grapes include p. 329 (8 December 1785) at the "Bunch of Grapes in State Street-at Brother Marstons," p. 318 (3 June 1784) at "Colº John Marstons State Street," and p. 331 (1 March 1786) for quoted reference. See Goss, 2:487 for location of Concert Hall. The *Proceedings* Vol. 2, indicate that by the 1790s most meetings were being held at Concert Hall. See *Proceedings* Vol. 2, p. 376 (2 March 1791) for quote on meeting days.

[96] See *Two Hundred and Fifty Years*, p. 7 for account of the union of the two Grand Lodges. See *Proceedings* Vol. 1, p. 340 (2 March 1787); p. 341 (6 April 1787); p. 380 (5 December 1791), and p. 381 (5 March 1792). See p. 379 (24 June 1791) for Revere's election as Deputy Grand Master.

[97] See *Constitutions*, pp. 146, 152 for Revere's appointments as Deputy Grand Master and *Proceedings* Vol. 1, p. 311 (4 December 1783); p. 368 (June 1790); p. 369 (24 June 1790) and p. 379 (24 June 1791). See *Proceedings* Vol. 2, pp. 5-11 for Grand Lodge constitution. This is the same constitution which was adopted at the time of the Union of the Massachusetts Grand Lodge and St. John's Grand Lodge on 19 March 1792. See *Proceedings* Vol. 2, pp. 60-61, 64-65 for Revere's election (8 and 12 December 1794).

[98] See *Proceedings* Vol. 2, p. 9 "Constitution" for Lodge meeting days. See p. 92 for reference to Chaplain (12 December 1796), and pp. 72-73 for feast days (8 and 24 June 1795).

[99] See *Proceedings* Vol. 2, pp. 28-29 for Constitution Book (10 December 1792); pp. 82 and 88 for Library Society (14 December 1795, 12 September 1796), and pp. 108-109 for revising Constitutions (13 September 1797). See Goss, 2:476 for reference to Revere writing "charges". See *Constitutions*, "Sanction" page, for list of compiling committee. See also Illustration 6 of this work. For Revere's quote about *Constitutions* "calculated with so much pains," see Paul Revere, "The Manner of Constituting a New Lodge," n.d., Grand Lodge of Massachusetts A.F. & A.M., Archives, Boston, Massachusetts.

[100] See *Two Hundred and Fifty Years*, p. 21 for list of Lodges chartered by Revere. See also Appendix 4. See *Proceedings* Vol. 2, p. 95 (22 December 1796);

p. 98 (13 March 1797), and pp. 78–79 (9 September 1795). For letters to and from Nantucket, see Paul Revere to Samuel Barrett, 27 August 1797, and Brother Hussey Secy to Coll. Paul Revere, 4 September 1797, Grand Lodge of Massachusetts A.F. & A.M., Archives, Boston, Massachusetts.

[101] See Paul Revere, "The Manner of Constituting a New Lodge" for quote on candidates. For quote on "worthless and profane," see Paul Revere to the Revd. George Richards, 1807(?), Grand Lodge of Masssachusetts A.F. & A.M., Archives, Boston, Massachusetts. See *Proceedings* Vol. 2, p. 96 for February 1797 Committee (23 February 1797); pp. 104–107 for problems with Harmonic Lodge (26 and 28 June 1797).

[102] See Goss, 2:479–485 for account of cornerstone laying. See *Proceedings* Vol. 2, pp. 74–76 (4 July 1795) for the order of procession, stone inscription and short description of the event.

[103] *Ibid.*

[104] See Goss, 2:483–485, for Revere's address. Revere's handwritten copy of the Cornerstone Speech is in the Grand Lodge of Massachusetts A.F. & A.M., Archives, Boston, Massachusetts. See *Proceedings* Vol. 2, p. 75 (4 July 1795) for reference to coins under the stone.

[105] See Ralph J. Pollard, *Famous American Freemasons* (Silver Spring, Md: Masonic Service Association, 15 October 1971), p. 6 for reference to Washington and cornerstone. See *Proceedings* Vol. 1, p. 284 for quotes from the letter from Pennsylvania (1 September 1780). See p. 284 (22 September 1780) and pp. 285–86 (1 December 1780) for additional references to a Grand Master General. For final decision of the Grand Lodge and long quoted passage, see pp. 288–89 (12 January 1781).

[106] See *Constitutions* for dedication to Washington. See *Proceedings* Vol. 2, p. 27 for references to sending the book to Washington (10 December 1792); pp. 34–35 for Washington's letter of reply (11 March 1793) and pp. 96, 101–102 for committee to write to Washington (13 March and 12 June 1797). See Goss, 2:485–87 for text of 1797 letter to Washington.

[107] For quote on Revere's "abilities in the masonic art" see *Proceedings* Vol. 2, p. 111 (11 December 1797). The *Proceedings* do not include the text of the Address. For text of Address, see Paul Revere, "Address to the Grand Lodge." See *Two Hundred and Fifty Years*, p. 7, "Union" for number of Lodges in 1792.

[108] For reference to committee formed, see *Proceedings*, Vol. 2, p. 111 (11 December 1797). For text of address, see Paul Revere, "Address to the Grand Lodge."

[109] Paul Revere, "Address to the Grand Lodge." See *Proceedings* Vol. 2, p. 117 (27 December 1797).

[110] For Revere's committees, see *Proceedings* Vol. 2 pp. 112–113 about letter from England (11 December 1797); p. 124 (17 January 1798); pp. 125–27 about compensating Harris (12 March 1798); p. 136 (10 December 1798); p. 142 (10 June 1799); pp. 145–46, 151 (9 December 1799).

[111] See Goss, 2:485–87 for text of letter to Washington (21 March 1797). For references to William Bentley, Salem and quotes about mourning and badges, see William Bentley, *The Diary of William Bentley, D.D. Pastor of the East Church, Salem, Massachusetts*, 2 vols. (Salem, Massachusetts: The Essex Institute, 1905–1907), 2:325–27.

[112] See Goss, 2:487–90 for text of letter to Mrs. Washington (11 January 1800). See *Proceedings* Vol. 2, pp. 156–57 (8 January 1800) for information on committees and funeral procession.

[113] For quotes, see *Proceedings* Vol. 2, pp. 157–60 (11 February 1800) for account of funeral service. See "Masonic Funeral Solemnities," (Portsmouth, N.H.), *The United States Oracle of the Day*, 22 February 1800, Grand Lodge of Massachusetts A.F. & A.M., Archives, Boston, Massachusetts, for an account

identical to that which appears in the *Proceedings*. For account of funeral service see Forbes, pp. 395–96.

[114] See *Proceedings* Vol. 2, pp. 157–60 (11 February 1800) for account of funeral service, including long quote about urn and quotes beginning "a blaze of chaste portraits . . ." and "returned to the State House . . ." See Goss, 2:493 for inscription on white urn. See William Bentley, *Diary*, 2:329 (11 February 1800) for account of service and quotes beginning "accomodated to . . ." and "above seven hours."

[115] See William Bentley, *Diary*, 2:329–30 for account of supper and quotes (11 February 1800); 2:426 for description of Revere as "enterprising mechanic" (19 April 1802). For references to bell see 2:374 (29 May 1801) and 2:363 (26 January 1801). See Forbes, pp. 396–99 for description of supper and personalities. For references to Revere's engravings for Isaiah Thomas see "Paul Revere, Wastebook."

[116] See William Bentley *Diary*, 2:330–31 (16, 22 and 23 February 1800) for quote "the day of . . ." For Grand Lodge committees and quotes see *Proceedings* Vol. 2, p. 168 (9 June 1800) and p. 403–405 (13 March 1809). For account of Revere housing the urn on Charter Street, see Forbes, pp. 400–401. See Goss, 2:493–95 for 1809 Committee and quotes. For copy of original resolve to Revere in 1809 and quote "permit them to remain . . ." see John Proctor Gd. Secretary to Paul Revere, Esq. 15 March 1809, Grand Lodge of Massachusetts A.F. & A.M., Archives, Boston, Massachusetts. This resolve is also included in Goss in full.

[117] See *Proceedings* Vol. 2, p. 168 for committee report (8 June 1800), p. 180 for reference to a "suitable inscription" (9 March 1801) and p. 549 (14 December 1812) for first reference to the mahogany cabinet in an inventory of Lodge possessions. See Appendix 5, note 40 for additional information on the cabinet. Although the *Proceedings* for 9 March 1801 recorded that the Committee appointed to procure the urn would report at the next meeting, there is no further reference to the gold urn in the published volume of Grand Lodge minutes. See Goss, 2:490–492 for description of urn and inscription and 2:489–90 for letter to Mrs. Washington with quotes beginning "Golden Urn . . ." and "cherished as . . ." The Golden Urn is preserved at the Grand Lodge of Massachusetts, A.F. & A.M., Boston, Massachusetts. The fate of the white urn is not known.

[118] See Goss, 2:531–32 for Revere's businesses after 1800; 2:556 for reference to buying Canton site, and 2:561 about gale of 1804 and State House Dome. See Forbes, pp. 407–10 for copper mill and quote about living in country and Joseph Warren. See p. 411 for gale of 1804. See William Bentley, *Diary*, 2:426 for Revere foundry description (19 April 1802).

[119] See Goss, 2:554–55 for description of Charter Street Home, and 2:493–94 for reference to white urn in 1809. See Forbes, pp. 400–401 for Charter Street Home; p. 411 for 1804 gale; p. 412 for reference to summers at Canton, and pp. 417–19 for a poem Revere wrote about "Canton Dale." See *Proceedings* Vol. 2, p. 239 (11 June 1804); pp. 244–45 (10 September 1804); pp. 295, 298 (28 and 31 October 1805). Paul Revere's attendance at Lodge meetings is difficult to determine after 1800. The general assumption is being made here that Revere greatly diminished his masonic activities in preference to his business involvements. This decision is due to the lack of records and is based more on what the existing records do *not* say. The printed minutes of the Grand Lodge, which faithfully list Lodge officers present, indicate that Revere was not holding any offices in the Grand Lodge after that of Master in 1794–1797. The minutes rarely record other members who attended, although reference is occasionally made to "Past Grand Officers" without listing specific names. The few times that "Past Grand Masters" are listed, Revere's name is not

among them. It is possible that more masons attended the meetings than were listed in the minutes, but it is just as likely that Revere was attending very few meetings during these years. The several specific instances mentioned here are among the only times that Revere's name even appears in the minutes, which seems to indicate a considerable decrease in masonic activity. Revere's standing in Rising States Lodge is even more obscure, since no minutes survive for the Lodge after 1784–1785. The existing information about Revere's offices in that Lodge has come from two manuscripts of "Return of Officers" dating prior to 1790, as well as from references to Rising States Lodge elections in the Grand Lodge *Proceedings*. Although representatives of Rising States Lodge attended Grand Lodge meetings until 1809, there were no other election reports for Rising States Lodge in the Grand Lodge *Proceedings* beyond the few instances mentioned here. Consequently, it is not known who served as officers in the Lodge during this period. Although 1793 is the last year for which evidence exists that Revere held an office in Rising States Lodge, he could have held offices in later years. As with the Grand Lodge, it is likely that Revere decreased his activities in Rising States Lodge while he concentrated on his business in Canton.

[120] See *Proceedings* Vol. 2, pp. 244–45 for committee and charter dates (10 September 1804), and pp. 413–15, 418–23 for admittance rank of St. Andrew's Lodge (11 September, 11 December 1809). When the two Grand Lodges joined in 1792, forming the new "Grand Lodge . . . for the Commonwealth of Massachusetts," St. John's became the first lodge under its jurisdiction, by virtue of its 1733 founding date. For a list of Lodges chartered from 1733, see *Two Hundred and Fifty Years*, pp. 16–17.

[121] See *Proceedings* Vol. 2, p. 436 (12 March 1810); pp. 438–39 (11 June 1810); pp. 450–51 (10 December 1810). The content of the complaint written by Rising States Lodge to the Grand Lodge was not recorded in the printed minutes. In the absence of minutes for Rising States Lodge, the account of the dissolution is taken solely from the minutes of the Grand Lodge, which was naturally biased against Rising States throughout most of the affair.

[122] See *Proceedings* Vol. 2, pp. 492–95 (9 September 1811). On this date "the committee appointed to take into consideration the late conduct of the Rising States Lodge, to trace the causes that led to its unprecedented dissolution, and to report what means would be most advisable for the Grand Lodge to adopt on this important occasion, have attended to the duty assigned them and respectfully submit the following . . ." They reported on the financial condition of the Lodge from at least 1788, on the yea and nay voters, and on the April summons.

[123] *Proceedings* Vol. 2, pp. 494–97 (9 September 1811).

[124] *Proceedings* Vol. 2, pp. 496–97 (9 September 1811). The committee takes the opportunity here to expound upon the charity fund and its use.

[125] See *Proceedings* Vol. 2, pp. 497–98 (9 September 1811) for conclusions reached by the Committee about the motives of Rising States Lodge, and p. 495 for testimony of Tuckerman.

[126] See *Proceedings* Vol. 2, p. 498 for quote beginning "purity of their principles . . ." (9 September 1811); p. 531 (9 March 1812); pp. 533–35 (8 June 1812) for Paul Revere quote; p. 541–42 (14 September 1812); pp. 552–55 (14 December 1812); p. 563 (8 March 1813); p. 567 (10 June 1813); p. 569 (13 September 1813); p. 574 (13 December 1813).

[127] For references to Revere and bells, see William Bentley, *Diary*, 2:374 (29 May 1801) and 2:426 (19 April 1802). See Paul Revere to the Revd. George Richards, 1807(?). See note 119 for a discussion of Revere's involvement with the Lodges after 1800.

[128] See "Paul Revere, Wastebooks." For a listing of the masonic items made

by Paul Revere, with a description of sources, see Appendix 5 of this work. For information on Paul Revere's father and Paul's youth, see Forbes, pp. 1–11, 39–41. Revere's father was originally named Apollos Rivoire, later changing his name to Paul Revere.

[129] For description of the goldsmith shop, see Forbes, pp. 34–35, 39–40. See Ruth L. Friedman, "Artisan to Entrepreneur: The Business Life of Paul Revere," (Boston, Spring 1978), pp. 13–16, 44, for a description of Paul Revere's various businesses and his customers, hereafter cited as "Friedman". A copy can be found at the Paul Revere House Library. See "Paul Revere, Wastebooks," 3 January 1761, 24 February 1762, 2 March 1762, 5 March 1762 for masonic medals. See also Appendix 5 for a list of masonic items made by Paul Revere.

[130] For reference to lodges in 1776, see Vaughn, p. 11. Vaughn estimates the masonic membership at between 1,500 and 5,000 from a total population of 2,500,000. For Boston population figures see Walter Muir Whitehill, *Boston, A Topographical History* (Cambridge, Massachusetts: The Belknap Press of Harvard University Press, 1959), pp. 37–38. See Friedman, pp. 14, 44 for references to customers. Friedman also includes an "Inventory of Paul Revere's Customers" from his ledgers 1763–1810, pp. 50–60. For the purposes of masonic identification, this writer also compiled a sampling of Revere's customers from his two "Wastebooks," 1761–1797. The list includes names which Friedman's list did not, and vice versa. This sampling of customers was created by recording every customer for the years 1761–62, 1765, 1770–71, 1775, 1780, 1783, 1787, 1790, 1793 and 1796. The Revere Family Papers at the Massachusetts Historical Society also contain an "Account Ledger for the Workshop at Boston 1761–1788" Microfilm Roll 7, Volume 13, which begins with several references from the goldsmith shop in 1761 and then skips to 1783. The remaining accounts appear to have been kept for Revere's hardware store, which opened in 1783. The ledger begins with an alphabetized listing of customers that includes approximately seventy-two complete names. These names from the hardware store ledger have also been included in the customer sampling and, for the most part, are persons who also appear in the goldsmith shop Wastebooks. This hardware store ledger will hereafter be cited as "Paul Revere, Account Ledger." For more information on the identification of masonic customers, see Appendix 5.

[131] Appendix 5 contains a list of documented masonic artifacts made by Paul Revere. See the introduction to Appendix 5 which explains why the list of nearly forty orders is probably not complete. See Henry N. Flynt and Martha Gandy Fales, *The Heritage Foundation Collection of Silver With Biographical Sketches of New England Silversmiths, 1625–1825* (Old Deerfield, Massachusetts: The Heritage Foundation, 1968) pp. 143–364, for silversmiths who were working in Boston during Revere's day. Out of approximately eighty craftsmen listed as goldsmiths, jewelers, clock and watchmakers, and engravers who were working during Revere's goldsmith period, this writer could identify a probable masonic connection for no more than fifteen craftsmen. The eighty craftsmen were researched in the same sources used to identify the masonic affiliations of Revere's customers (consult Appendix 5). Of note are the Hurd brothers, Benjamin and Nathaniel, who were both masons and well-known goldsmiths and engravers. See Flynt and Fales, p. 255. Benjamin Hurd is known to have made masonic engravings. Nathaniel Hurd was among the names in Revere's Wastebooks.

[132] This information is taken from Appendix 5, containing the list of masonic customers, as well as from the notes to that Appendix. See Appendix 5 for more details and sources. For the information quoted concerning Revere's involvement with Tyrian Lodge, see Earle J. T. Merchant, Secy., Tyrian Lodge

to Librarian, Grand Lodge of Massachusetts, 22 April 1967, in the folder "Paul Revere Project," Grand Lodge of Massachusetts A.F. & A.M., Library, Boston, Massachusetts. According to this letter, Revere served as proxy until 1777 when he was elected Master of St. Andrew's Lodge, at which time he asked to be replaced. The Grand Lodge *Proceedings*, Vol. 1 also indicate when Revere was serving as proxy for Tyrian Lodge. Friedman, pp. 13–14, 20, 28, discusses the personal nature of Revere's goldsmith business, drawing a contrast to his later industrial ventures, such as the foundry and the copper-rolling mill, which relied increasingly upon mail orders from customers whom Revere never knew personally. The three customers from Lodges in Maine were James Avery of Warren Lodge in Machias, James Eveleth of Lincoln Lodge in Wiscassett, and David How of Hancock Lodge in Penobscot. All three were made masons or were members of St. Andrew's Lodge before they became associated with the Lodges in Maine. It is not unusual for masons to be associated with more than one Lodge at a time. See Appendix 5 for details on masonic customers.

[133] For jewels see "Paul Revere, Wastebooks," 28 July 1781, 9 January 1782, 18 March 1784, 26 June 1784, 7 July, 25 July and 5 September 1797. See 1 June 1792 for "Jenks" and 15 June 1773 for Tyrian Lodge. For "Cross Keys" see 15 September 1772 and 15 June 1773. For "Cross-pens" see 4 April 1787. For prices of Revere's jewels, see 9 January 1782, 18 March 1784 and 5 September 1797. All of the above information, as well as additional documentation from sources other than the Wastebooks, is included in Appendix 5.

[134] For information on masonic items other than jewels, see Appendix 5 and notes. See Brigham, Clarence C., *Paul Revere's Engravings* (New York: Atheneum, 1969), pp. 4, 124–25.

[135] For individual customers mentioned, see "Paul Revere, Wastebooks," 3 January 1761, 19 November 1762, 1 February 1763, 15 September 1772, 4 April 1783 and 31 October 1789. See Appendix 5 for masonic customers and masonic items purchased, and the notes of Appendix 5 for details on customers and sources.

[136] The random list of items made by Revere in his goldsmith shop was gathered from "Paul Revere, Wastebooks," 1761–1797. In this source, see September 1783, for "Stock Ready Made in the Cases." See Friedman, pp. 14, 19. Forbes includes a drawing of a house probably similar to one that Revere rented at the head of Clark's Wharf. See plates between pages 34 and 35.

[137] For patterns of business during the Revolutionary period see "Paul Revere, Wastebook," 1761–1783. See Friedman, pp. 7–9 for a discussion of the pace of Revere's business. For military rank see Forbes, pp. 305, 307.

[138] See Goss, 2:516 about the letter from Paul Revere to his cousin John Rivoire. Also see pp. 527–28 for mention of the hardware store. In a letter dated 5 September 1783, Revere wrote that "I have already opened a large store of hardware directly opposite where Liberty Tree stood." This letter, which was written to Mr. Frederick William Geyer, is in the Revere Papers at the Massachusetts Historical Society. Friedman, p. 19 mentions that the silver shop was run concurrently with the hardware store. She states that Paul Revere, Sr. gave most of his time to the hardware store, leaving the silver shop to Paul Jr. Forbes, pp. 357–58 states just the opposite. She felt that since Paul Revere, Sr. was making "a great deal" of the silver, then his son, Paul Jr., must have been conducting most of the hardware store business. Judging from the types of items being made in the latter years of the goldsmith business, it does not seem that Paul Revere, Sr. left the shop entirely to his son. For location of the hardware store and the 1786 move and quote, see Forbes, pp. 361–62. For 1785 inventory see Paul Revere Cash Journal 1785–1786, 15 February 1785, Revere Family Papers, Microfilm Roll 11, Volume 32,

Massachusetts Historical Society, Boston, Massachusetts. This is a "cash journal showing daily sales and cash on hand for the workshop at Boston." From the entries, this seems to be a journal for the hardware store. For the alphabetized customer listing from the hardware store, see Paul Revere, Account Ledger. For the sources utilized to identify masons, see the introduction to Appendix 5.

[139] See Loose Manuscripts 1746–1801, Revere Family Papers, Massachusetts Historical Society, Boston, Massachusetts, for the following receipts: "August 22 1768 Mr. Paul Revere to Bouve and Stodder" and "April 23 1776 Cor.el Paul Revere to Gibb Bouve." See same source for "January 17, 1783 Col Paul Revere to Saml Danforth." See "Paul Revere, Wastebooks," 22 August 1768 for reference to Mrs. Marett. For sources of masonic affiliation, see introduction to Appendix 5.

[140] For references to DeFrance see Forbes, pp. 396, 400 and "Paul Revere, Wastebooks," 27 May 1780, 27 and 28 August 1780 and 28 August 1781. For references to Dunkerley in the Wastebooks see 19 April 1784, 19 January 1785, 19 July 1785, 19 October 1785, and 19 January 1786. For information about Dunkerley also see Forbes, pp. 400 and 459. Depending upon the source consulted, the spelling of his name varies. Revere called him "Dunkerley" in his Wastebooks, while the Rising States Lodge Minutes list him most frequently as "Dunckerly" or "Dunckerley". Forbes refers to him simply as "Dunkerly". For quote about Dunkerley, see his notice in the December 1784, *Independent Chronicle*. Reference to this notice is included in "Paul Revere House Data 1770–1800," a chronology of pertinent data compiled from the Revere Family Papers, tax lists, deeds and city directories. This chronology can be found in the "Paul Revere Papers," a typewritten volume containing an inventory of the Revere Papers from the Massachusetts Historical Society. The volume is located at the Paul Revere House Library. For reference to George DeFrance and Friendship Lodge see *Proceedings* Vol. 1, pp. 280, 282–83. By 1 September 1780, DeFrance had been expelled from Friendship Lodge for "malconduct." By 7 September 1781, *Proceedings* Vol. 1, p. 293, the Grand Lodge dismissed the charges. A man by this name was also made a mason in St. Andrew's Lodge in January 1782.

[141] According to Vaughn, p. 4, so few local studies have been done that it is still difficult to "develop an accurate national profile of the typical Mason during the period between the American Revolution and the beginning of the Antimasonic crusade, 1826–1827." He concludes that, based on the limited studies, early nineteenth century masons tended to be prosperous and politically active men who frequently assumed leadership positions. Vaughn refers to Lipson, who found that masons tended to be mobile and often leaders of religious and political dissent. Vaughn also mentions Kutolowski, who discusses early masonry in Genesee County, New York from 1809–1847.

[142] See William Bentley, *Diary*, 2:190 for quote (25 June 1796). See also Paul Revere to Francis Oliver, 1 September 1817, Grand Lodge of Massachusetts A.F. & A.M., Boston, Massachusetts. For Paul Revere's death, see Forbes, pp. 445–46.

[143] For quote, see Paul Revere, "Address to the Grand Lodge."

APPENDIX 1

A LIST OF MEMBERS OF SAINT ANDREW'S LODGE

The following is from the *Centennial Memorial of the Lodge of St. Andrew* (Boston: Printed by vote of the Lodge St. Andrew, 1870), pp. 241–42. According to this source, the list was "made at communication held in Royal Exchange Tavern, King Street, Boston, the 2d Thursday of January, 1762." The first reference to such a list appears in the minutes of St. Andrew's Lodge in late December 1761, when it was "voted unan: That a List of this Lodge [be] Printed with the Names + Occupation." The exact date of this meeting is not given, but it was probably the source of the January 1762 list. An updated list, which has not survived, is mentioned on December 9, 1763 when it was "voted to have a New List of the Lodge Reprinted." The following list includes occupations and residences.

George Bray	Baker	Williams' Court, Corn-hill
William Burbeck	Carver	New Salutation Alley
James Graham	Chairmaker	Head of Clark's Wharf
Samuel Peck	Glazier	By Hallowell's Ship Yard
Thomas Milliken	Bricklayer	Fish Street
John Jenkins	Baker	Near Mill Bridge
Moses Deshon	Auctioneer	Dock Square
Joseph Webb, Jr.	Ship Chandler	Head of Oliver's Dock
Samuel Barrett	Sailmaker	Pulling's Wharf
Ambrose Sloper	Shipwright	Battery March
Paul Revere	Gold Smith + Engraver	Fish Street
Thomas Urann	Ship Joiner	By Hallowell's Ship Yard
Phillip Lewis	Merchant	Middle Street
George Jefferds	Sugar Refiner	Atkinson Street
Nathaniel Hitchborn	Boat Builder	Near Draw Bridge
Increase Blake	Tin Plate Worker	West End Faneuil Hall
William Palfrey	Merchant	Town Dock

Samuel Moody	Merchant	Old York
Edward Potter	Cooper	Milk Street
John Whitten	Gun Smith	By Hallowell's Ship Yard
William McAlpine	Stationer + Bookbinder	Marlboro' Street
James Nicolls	House-wright	Atkinson Street
Josiah Flagg	Jeweller	Fish Street
John Hoffins	Sugar Refiner	New Boston
Richard Pulling	Merchant	Fish Street
Thomas Crafts	Japanner + Painter	Opposite the Great Tree
Joseph Warren	Physician	Corn-hill
William Gould	Merchant	King Street
Elisha Callender	Sail Maker	New Boston
William Ham	Merchant	West Indies
John Marlton	Merchant	West Indies
Henry Stanbridge	Painter	Cross Street
Edward Burbeck	Carver	New Salutation Street
James Seward	Gun Smith	Fish Street
Ezra Collins	Hat Maker	Fish Street

SEAFARING MEMBERS

Capt. Edward Jarvis
" Henry Wells
" Seth Chipman
" Phillip Marett
" Peter Doyle
" William Wingfield
" Israel Obear
" John Phillips
" Hugh Brown

Capt. Wait Gray
" Walter Kerr
" Ambrose Ferrell
" Edw'd Cailleteau
" Philip Tabor
" Gilbert Ash
" Alexander Inglish
" Thomas Webster
" William Bell

APPENDIX 2

LODGE OFFICES HELD BY PAUL REVERE

The following list has been compiled primarily from the Lodge minutes of St. Andrew's, Rising States and the Massachusetts Grand Lodge. Documentation on each item is included where these positions are mentioned in the main body of the book. A list of Grand Lodge positions that includes Revere can also be found in the *Most Worshipful Grand Lodge of Ancient Free and Accepted Masons of the Commonwealth of Massachusetts, Directory 1981*, pp. 108–111.

Several questionable dates have been indicated. No one knows precisely when Paul Revere was "passed" to the second degree of Fellow Craft, although it has been suggested that he received the degree on January 8, 1761, because several masons were passed at that meeting. Although Revere was present at the meeting on January 8, six people were specifically listed as having received the second degree, and Revere was not one of them. Concerning Revere's election as Junior Deacon of St. Andrew's Lodge for 1762, the election took place at a meeting of "Special Occasion" sometime between December 10 and December 24, 1761, according to its placement in the minutes. The meeting itself bears no date. The list of Rising States Lodge positions was pieced together from fragmentary evidence and is probably incomplete, since minutes do not exist beyond 1785. Revere could have held more positions in Rising States Lodge than those which are recorded here. In the Grand Lodge, Paul Revere may also have been Deputy Grand Master from June 1790, since he appears in that position at every meeting until the next election. It is never specifically stated who was chosen Deputy Grand Master for this year. The officers are listed in *Proceedings* Vol. 1, pp. 367–68 (3 June 1790), with the Deputy Grand Master as the only officer not mentioned by name, so Revere could have been chosen at this time.

ST. ANDREW'S LODGE

September 4, 1760—Initiated as an Entered Apprentice
January 8, 1761(?)—Possibly Passed to Fellow Craft Degree

January 27, 1761—Raised to Master Mason Degree
December 1761(?)—Election—Junior Deacon for 1762
November 30, 1763—Election—Junior Warden for 1764
November 30, 1764—Election—Senior Warden for 1765
November 30, 1767—Election—Secretary for 1768
November 30, 1768—Election—Secretary for 1769
December 11, 1769—Royal Arch Mason—St. Andrew's Chapter.
November 30, 1770—Election—Master for 1771
December 2, 1777—Election—Master for 1778
November 30, 1778—Election—Master for 1779
November 30, 1780—Election—Master for 1781
November 30, 1781—Election—Master for 1782
February 5, 1784—Dismissed from St. Andrew's Lodge

RISING STATES LODGE (St. Andrew's Lodge)

February 1784—New Lodge formed—Revere as Treasurer
May 31, 1784—Election—Treasurer for 1784–1785
February 28, 1785—Revere serves as Master (after Master resigns)
June 2, 1785—Election—Treasurer for 1785–1786
May 2, 1787—Election—Master for 1787–1788
By May 26, 1788—Election—Master for 1788–1789
By June 2, 1791—Election—Master for 1791–1792
By December 10, 1792—Election—Master for 1792–1793
1810–1811—Rising States Lodge dissolves.

MASSACHUSETTS (PROVINCIAL) GRAND LODGE
DEC. 27, 1769–MARCH 8, 1777

September, 1769—Accepts commission to be Senior Grand Deacon
December 27, 1769—Election—Senior Grand Deacon for 1770
By March 1, 1771—Serving as Senior Grand Deacon for 1771
December 6, 1771—Voted one of two "G. Deacons" for 1772
December 4, 1772—Election—Senior Grand Deacon for 1773
December 3, 1773—Election—Senior Grand Deacon for 1774

MASSACHUSETTS (INDEPENDENT) GRAND LODGE
MARCH 8, 1777–MARCH 5–19, 1792

March 8, 1777—Election—Junior Grand Warden for 1777
December 4, 1777—Continued as Junior Grand Warden for 1778
December 4, 1778—Election—Junior Grand Warden for 1779
December 3, 1779—Election—Senior Grand Warden for 1780
December 1, 1780—Election—Senior Grand Warden for 1781
March 1, 1782—Election—Senior Grand Warden for 1782
December 6, 1782—Election—Senior Grand Warden for 1783

December 4, 1783—Election—Deputy Grand Master for 1784–June 1785
June 1790(?)—Election—Deputy Grand Master for ensuing year
June 24, 1791—Election—Deputy Grand Master for ensuing year

MASSACHUSETTS GRAND LODGE SINCE UNION OF MARCH 5–19, 1792

December 27, 1794—Installed as Grand Master
March 9, 1795–December 27, 1797—Grand Master

APPENDIX 3

VOTE OF ST. ANDREW'S LODGE 1784

On January 22, 1784, St. Andrew's Lodge took a vote to determine whether it would remain loyal to Scotland, or declare its allegiance to the Massachusetts Grand Lodge. The following is a record of how the members voted. The minority, who voted for the Massachusetts Grand Lodge, formed Rising States Lodge soon after. This list can be found in the Minutes of St. Andrew's Lodge, 22 January 1784, and in the *Centennial Memorial of the Lodge of St. Andrew* (Boston: Printed by vote of the Lodge of St. Andrew, 1870), p. 244.

For Grand Lodge of Scotland	For Massachusetts Grand Lodge
Samuel Barrett	Nathaniel Fellows
Wm. Burbeck	Paul Revere
Thomas Urann	Jona. Stodder
Asa Stodder	John Boit
James Carter	Cornelius Fellows
William Bell	Benj. Coolidge
John Symmes	David Howe
Elisha Sigourney	J. Dunckerly
Elias Thomas	John T. Morgan
Edward Rumney	Robert McElroy
Alexander Thomas	R. Hichborn
Manassah Marston	Amos Lincoln
Samuel Moore	Levi Hearsey
James Graham	Simon Hall
Isaac Snow	Daniel Rea
Jacob Dunnels	Enoch Pond
Thomas Wells	Joshua Davis
Timothy Green	Joseph Webber
Thomas Dakin	Daniel Ingersoll
Joseph Bush	Thomas Russell

Wm. Peak
Benj. White
Jona. W. Edes
Thomas Knox
John Whitten
John Rand
Gibbons Bouve
Moses Dorran
Samuel Gore
Freeman Pulsifer

Thomas P. Low
Norton Brailsford
Nathaniel Willis

APPENDIX 4

LODGES CHARTERED BY PAUL REVERE AS GRAND MASTER 1795–1797*

NAME OF LODGE	LOCATION	DATE OF CHARTER
Republican	Greenfield	February 7, 1795
Evening Star	Lee	June 9, 1795
Middlesex	Framingham	June 13, 1795
Cincinnatus	Great Barrington	December 9, 1795
King Hiram's	Provincetown	December 14, 1795
Kennebec	Hallowell, Maine	March 15, 1796
Fayette	Charlton	March 15, 1796 (Extinct)
Washington	Roxbury (now Lexington)	March 17, 1796
Columbian	Boston	June 9, 1796
Harmony	Northfield	June 15, 1796
Union	Dorchester	June 16, 1796
Thomas	Palmer	December 13, 1796
St. Paul	Ayer	January 26, 1797
Jerusalem	Northampton	June 13, 1797
Adams	Wellfleet	June 13, 1797 (Revived)
Tuscan	Columbia, Maine	June 13, 1797 (Extinct)
Bristol	N. Attleboro	June 14, 1797
Fellowship	Bridgewater	June 15, 1797
Corinthian	Concord	June 16, 1797
Meridian Sun	Brookfield	September 13, 1797 (Revived)
Olive Branch	Millbury	September 14, 1797
Montgomery	Milford	September 16, 1797
Meridian	Natick	December 10, 1797

*This list is taken from The Grand Lodge of Massachusetts, *Two Hundred and Fifty Years of Massachusetts Masonry* (Boston: Rapid Service Press, 1983), p. 21.

APPENDIX 5

MASONIC ITEMS MADE BY PAUL REVERE

The following is a list of items that Paul Revere made for masonic use between 1761 and 1801. A variety of sources were used to compile this list. Most of the items were found in "Paul Revere, Wastebooks," 1761–1797, two volumes produced while Revere was working as a Boston goldsmith. Unless otherwise noted, the dated items with prices are from the Wastebooks. Clarence C. Brigham examines Revere's masonic engravings through surviving examples and references to the Wastebooks. In his work, *Paul Revere's Engravings* (New York: Athenaeum, 1969), Brigham discusses several Revere engravings which are not in the Wastebooks, and those have been included in this list. References made in primary sources, such as Lodge Minutes and Paul Revere's Rising States Lodge Record Book, have also been included. These primary sources are located at the Grand Lodge of Massachusetts, A.F. & A.M., Boston, Massachusetts. A partial listing of Revere's masonic items from the Wastebooks was included in Charles Messer Stow, "Paul Revere, Craftsman," in *Transactions of the American Lodge of Research, Free and Accepted Masons* (New York: Grand Lodge of Free and Accepted Masons, State of New York, 18 December 1947–31 May 1949), 5:13–20. This Appendix utilizes Stow's list, including references from the Wastebooks which he omitted.

Several sources have been used to identify the Lodges and individual customers in Revere's Wastebooks. The Grand Lodge of Massachusetts' Library contains lists of members and initiates for the Lodges of St. John and St. Andrew. See *History of St. John's Lodge of Boston* (Boston: privately printed, 1917), pp. 199–232, 245–262, and *Commemoration of Lodge of Saint Andrew*, pp. 273–301. Also in the Grand Lodge Library, see Parker, Index 1733–1800. This is a manuscript source, being a bound volume with handwritten entries on early masons from all Massachusetts Lodges, arranged alphabetically. Another source of information about Massachusetts masons is the membership file at the Grand Secretary's office of the Grand Lodge of Massachusetts. This office keeps cards on all Massachusetts masons, both active and inactive. Unfortunately, the early Grand Lodge records were destroyed by fire, so that the current files have been reconstructed. They are helpful, but not complete. Where not specified, information about Lodge membership included in the accompanying notes has been gathered from the above named sources. For the charter dates of Lodges, see *Two Hundred and Fifty Years*, pp. 16–21. This source also contains biographical information on prominent masons.

Due to gaps in the available sources, the following list probably only partially represents Paul Revere's total masonic production. Even Revere's own Wastebooks are an incomplete record of all that he made, since many silver items exist today which have never been located in the Wastebooks. In the same way, Revere probably also did masonic work which he never recorded. Numerous such examples are already cited on this list. Revere did work for masons and Lodges without always indicating the masonic connection in his records, such as with the ladles made for Samuel Barrett. In several instances, the masonic use has been inferred from the description of the item. Several items with a questionable masonic connection have been indicated and discussed. This list primarily includes items which have been documented in Lodge minutes and in Revere's own records, along with some existing documented pieces. Many Lodges claim to own Revere artifacts, most of which have not been included here due to a lack of precise documentation. This writer welcomes any additional information on Paul Revere masonic items.

MASONIC ITEMS MADE BY PAUL REVERE

1761	January 3 Mr. James Grayham[1] To a Free Mason medal	0-13-4
1762	February 24 Mr. Richard Pulling[2] To a Masons medal for a Wach	0-9-0
	March 2 Mr. James Jackson[3] To a Masons Medal	0-12-0
	March 5 Mr. George Stacy[4] To a Masons Medal for Wach	0-9-0
Possibly Masonic	March 22 Mr. John Pulling Junr[5] To Cutting a Copper Plate for Notifications	1-4-0
	To 2 Hundred Notifications at 6/p. Hundd.	0-12-0

	October 14	
	St. Andrews Lodge[6]	
	"paid . . to Brother Rever for his Bill for £1.6.8 LM°"	
	November 19	
	Mr. Samuel Barrett[7]	
	To two Silver Punch Ladles w⁺4:0	1-8-0
	To the making at 16/ Each	1-12-0
	To two Wooding Handles	0-2-0
1766	November 14	
	Capt. Caleb Hopkins[8]	
	To Engraving a Copper Plate for Notifications for a Masons Lodge in Surinam	3-6-8
	To 500 prints from it at 6/8 pr Hudd.	1-13-4
Late 1760s(?)	Lodge No. 169 Ancient York Masons of Boston[9]	
	Notification Engraved and Signed by Revere	
1769	September 19	
	St. Andrew's Lodge "Voted . .: that the G. Lodge be provided with jewells made of any mettal under silver, + that the Lodge accept of Brother Revere's offer to make the jewells and wait for his pay, till the G. Lodge is in Cash to pay him."[10]	
1770	December 7	
	The Grand Lodge of Massachusetts "Voted that B^r Revere cut a seal for their G^d Lodge + that the money arising from the Charters of the Massa + Tyrian Lodge be pd him on acct."[11]	
1772	September 15	
	Mr. Simon Greenleaf, Newbury-port[12]	
	To Engraving a plate for Notifications	2-8-0
	To 300 Prints	0-18-0
	To a Floor Cloth	1-16-0
	To a P^r of Silver Cross Keys	0-18-0
	To a Frame & Glass for a picture	0-7-4
Possibly Masonic	September 24—Receipt[13]	
	"Boston Sep 24 1772 Received of Mr. Joseph Denison one Pound Sixteen Shillings + Eight pence in full for a Silver Seal + Stock. Paul Revere."	

Possibly Masonic	October (11)? Mr. Simon Greenleaf[14] To a Silver Seal + : Stock	1-0-0
1773	June 15 The Tyrian Lodge[15] To Engraving a Plate for Summons To 400 Impressions To P Cross Keys To two Stewards Jewils	3-0-0 1-4-0 0-18-0 0-18-0
	1773(?) The Tyrian Lodge[16] Punch Ladle Engraved "Tyrian Lodge No. 1"	
	1773 or earlier[17] Revere engraved a large general copper plate certificate, with blanks to be filled in by the recipient.	
1780(?)	1780 or earlier[18] Revere engraved a small general copper plate certificate, with blanks to be filled in by the recipient.	
1781	July 28 Col. John Brooks[19] To a Sett of silver Jewels for Washington Lodge W 5oz To the Making	1-15-0 6-15-0
1782	January 9 Nath' Tracy Esq[20] To a sett of Silv Jewels for a Lodge W^{oz} 10 = 6 at [?]/ To making Mas^r + Warden Jew/ each 24/ To making Sec^y + Treas^r 20/ each To making Deac + Stewards 12/each	3-12-0 3-12-0 2-0-0 <u>2-8-0</u> 11-12-0
Possibly Masonic	March 6 From Jn Barrett, Springfield to Col^n Paul Revere ". . . desiring you would send me the Jewels up by the bearer, with a bill of the same, I send by the same hand seven pounds ten shillings as the sum you told me they wou'd amount to . . ."[21]	

	April 27	
	Doc John Blanchard[22]	
	To engraving a Copper Plate for Certificates	4-10-0
	To Printing 2 hr Impressions	0-16-0
1783	October 10	
	Doc John Warren[23]	
	To a Collar for a Masons Jewel	1-4-0
	December 12	
	St. Andrew's Lodge[24]	
	"Voted . . . that the Secy' supply the Lodge with blank summonses as many as he shall think necessary for the two following years."	
1784	January 14	
	King Solomon's Lodge at Charlestown[25]	
	To two Silver Ladles	2-16-0
	March	
Possibly Revere?	St. Andrew's Lodge/Rising States Lodge[26]	
	To Engraving Copper Plate for Summons	4-10-0
	To Printing 400 Impressions @ 8/	1-12-0
	March	
Possibly Revere?	St. Andrew's Lodge/Rising States Lodge[27]	
	To Silver Jewels for Mar, Wardn Trea^r, Sec^y Dea^n : 2 Steward + Tyler	13-10-0
	March 18	
	Lodge[28]	
	To Jewels	12-0-0
	June 26	
	Mr. James Avery[29]	
	To 5 Masons Jewls for Warren Lodge	9-0-0
	To printing 5 Certificates @ 1/	0-5-0
1784(?) Possibly Revere?	Rising States Lodge[30] Seal	
1787	April 4	
	Mr. Samuel W. Hunt[31]	
	To p Silver Cross pens	0-18-0
1792	June 1	
	Jenks[32]	
	To a Masons Jewel	0-10-0
	June 1	
	Mr. Eveleth[33]	
	To printing 12 paper + 12 parchment Certificates	1-2-0

1795		June 25—Receipt[34]	
		The Columbian Lodge to Paul Revere and Son	
		To the Masters Jewel	0-18-6
		To the S^r. Wardens Do:	1-0-0
		To the J^r. Wardens Do:	0-15-0
		To the Sec.^{y}.	1-2-6
		To the Treuseres	1-2-6
		To S^r. Decons	0-17-6
		To J^r. Decons	0-17-6
		To the Stewards	0-13-6
		To the - Do: -	0-13-6
		To the Tylors	0-12-0
			£ 8-12-7
1796		1796	
		Washington Lodge[35]	
		Twelve masonic officers jewels	
1796		May 18	
		Mr. David How[36]	
		To 12 Certificates	0-12-0
1797		July 7	
		South Hadley Lodge[37]	
		To a Sett of Silver Jewels	12-0-0
		July 25	
		Mr. Saml Dana[38]	
		To a Silver Sett Mason Jewell'	12-0-0
		Sept 5	
		Mr. Seth Smith Jr of Norton[39]	
		To a Silver Sett of Masons Jewels	12-0-0
1800–1801		Grand Lodge of Massachusetts Golden Urn[40]	

NOTES TO APPENDIX 5

[1] James Graham was initiated into St. Andrew's Lodge before 10 April 1756 and was elected to the office of Senior Deacon on 19 December 1760. He was a chairmaker, living at the head of Clark's Wharf.

[2] Richard Pulling was a Fish Street Merchant, initiated into St. Andrew's Lodge on 13 June 1761. According to Charles Messer Stow (p. 18), it was not uncommon for men to attach "trinkets" to their watch chains, including masonic medals.

[3] James Jackson appears as a member of St. John's Lodge in December 1762, and also as an initiate of St. Andrew's, 12 October 1769.

[4] The only record of George Stacy in the Grand Lodge files is as a Newburyport merchant who joined St. John's Lodge of that place between 1781 and 1787. If this is the same man who purchased the "Masons Medal" in 1762, he must have belonged to a Lodge prior to 1781. Although he is not recorded on the membership lists for St. John's or St. Andrew's Lodges, a George Stacey did attend the St. Andrew's Lodge meeting of 11 April 1765 as a visitor. It could be this George Stacey who purchased the masonic medal from Revere in 1762. It is not stated what Lodge he was representing.

[5] John Pulling, Jr. was a vestryman at the present Old North Church. He was also a member of St. Andrew's Lodge as early as 1761, and Philanthropic Lodge in Marblehead, chartered in 1760. Although not specified as a masonic notification, this plate could have been made for either Lodge. See Brigham p. 184 and *Two Hundred and Fifty Years,* p. 40.

[6] This item from the St. Andrew's Lodge Minutes is included only because it suggests that Revere did some sort of work for the Lodge. The minutes do not specify what service Revere performed for the Lodge at this time, nor are there any direct references in Revere's Wastebook to St. Andrew's Lodge during 1762. The minutes for St. Andrew's Lodge mention a seal at this period, although there is no evidence to document that Revere was the craftsman. The first reference to the seal appears on 12 February 1761 when it was "voted unam^y that a Seal be provided for the Lodge at the Expence of S^d Lodge." A second reference occurs in the month after the Lodge received Revere's bill. On 30 November 1762, the Lodge voted that "a press for the Seal be provided for the Use of the Lodge." While there is no direct connection between Revere's bill and this seal, it is interesting to speculate whether Revere might have made it, particularly since he had already made four masonic medals by 1762.

[7] Samuel Barrett is listed as a member of St. Andrew's Lodge, 10 July 1760. Although these ladles are not listed specifically as masonic items in Revere's Wastebook, Samuel Barrett did donate ladles to St. Andrew's Lodge. In the minutes of 30 November 1762, the Lodge thanked Brother Barrett "for donation of two Genteel Silver Ladles." Numbered "N°1" and "N°2," the ladles were engraved "The Gift of /B^r Sam^L Barrett to/St Andrew's Lodge/N°82/1762".

See *Paul Revere's Boston 1735–1818* (Boston: Museum of Fine Arts, 1975), p. 212 for photograph of the ladles. According to this source, Barrett was a known Son of Liberty and a successful businessman. The St. Andrew's Lodge List of Members for January, 1762, contains a Samuel Barrett who was a Sailmaker living on Pulling's Wharf.

[8] Caleb Hopkins became associated with St. Andrew's Lodge on 13 May 1762. He was also a Grand Lodge officer in 1770, 1773 and 1777. The Surinam Lodge was under the jurisdiction of St. John's Grand Lodge. New England traded with Surinam (Dutch Guiana), which supplied sugar and cocoa to the colonies. No copy of this notification exists. See Brigham, p. 185.

[9] According to Brigham, p. 185, this was "probably done in the late 1760's," although it does not appear in Revere's Wastebook. See Brigham, plate 60A, for photograph.

[10] See St. Andrew's Lodge Minutes, 19 September 1769. If Revere did make jewels for the Grand Lodge, they are no longer in existence. There was no reference to them in his Wastebook, which contained only five items for the period August 1769 to 1770, none of which were masonic.

[11] See *Proceedings* Vol. 1, pp. 233, 237. Presumably, Revere did make the seal because one year later, on 6 December 1771, it was "voted that the monies arising from the charter of the Tyrian + Massa Lodges be paid B^r Revere on Account." The Grand Lodge of Massachusetts A.F. & A.M., Archives, owns several seals which were possibly made by Revere, although no documentation exists. One is labeled "Seal of Anc. Grand Lodge Boston" which could be this early seal. According to Charles Messer Stow, pp. 19–20, Revere is credited with making the seal for the Grand Lodge. Stow does not specify whether this claim is based on the original reference in *Proceedings* or on the actual existence of the seal.

[12] Simon Greenleaf was a member of St. Peter's Lodge, Newburyport, 23 March 1772. Although Paul Revere's Wastebook does not specify this notification as masonic, Brigham contains a photograph of the notification which was made for St. Peter's Lodge by Revere in 1772. See Brigham, pp. 185–87, Plate 59. The cross keys may refer to the Lodge jewel for the office of Treasurer.

[13] This receipt is owned by the Grand Lodge of Massachusetts A.F. & A.M., Archives. Although there is no indication that this seal was masonic, the Grand Lodge attributes the purchase to the Union Lodge of Nantucket, Massachusetts. This item was not listed in Revere's Wastebook.

[14] See note 12 for probable identification.

[15] Tyrian Lodge was chartered in Gloucester, Massachusetts on 2 March 1770. Tyrian Lodge still owns the plate and several prints of this plate still exist. See Brigham, pp. 182, 187–88. According to the Tyrian Lodge, it currently owns three jewels—for the Master, Senior Warden and Junior Warden. In 1967, the Librarian of the Grand Lodge of Massachusetts wrote to the early Lodges inquiring whether they owned any Paul Revere artifacts. Tyrian Lodge responded in a letter written 22 April 1967. This letter can be found in a folder marked "Paul Revere Project" in the files of the Librarian of the Grand Lodge of Massachusetts. The letter was written by Earle J.T. Merchant, Secy., who quoted from a paper that he had written and delivered himself in March 1955 for the 175th anniversary of Tyrian Lodge. According to this paper, which he did not title, the first meeting of Tyrian Lodge took place on 9 March 1770. At that meeting, a bill from Paul Revere was read, charging the Lodge for one box, two candlesticks, painted flooring, a balloting box, truncheons and gilding, jewels, ribbon, a Book and twelve aprons. Mr. Merchant did not claim that all of these items were still owned by the Lodge, except for the three jewels and the engraved plate for notices. He did assert, however, that Revere also made a silver candelabra for the Lodge, along with the plate and

jewels in the 1955 paper. Revere's Wastebook does not contain any references to Tyrian Lodge jewels or candlesticks in 1770. Mr. Merchant did not provide any additional details about the 1955 paper or the sources he used in it.

[16] See Kathryn C. Buhler, *Paul Revere Goldsmith 1735–1818* (Boston, Massachusetts: Museum of Fine Arts), n.d., no. 18 for photo of ladle. This ladle is in the MFA collection. Taking her information from Revere's two Wastebooks, Buhler claims that "In 1773 Revere charged sundry items to the Tyrian Lodge in Gloucester. . ." but this writer could find no reference to the Tyrian Lodge in 1773 in Revere's Wastebook except for the one listed above (see 15 June 1773), which does not mention sundries or a ladle.

[17] According to Brigham, p. 188, many copies of the engraving still exist, the earliest dated print being from 3 February 1774. For photograph, see Brigham, Plate 61 or Illustration 10 in this work. Rather than being made for a particular Lodge, this certificate could have been purchased by any masonic customers.

[18] See Brigham, Plate 62, pp. 189, 191–92. Several copies of this engraving exist, the earliest dated copy being from 30 May 1780. According to the bottom right hand corner of the engraving, it was "Printed + Sold opposite Liberty Stump Boston," which would be near the corner of Washington and Essex Streets. Revere owned the "Liberty Stump" property from the Revolutionary period until 1786, when he moved his shop. There is no specific mention of this engraving in Revere's Wastebook. There are practically no entries between 1 April 1775 and 19 December 1778, and the entries are relatively few until November 1780. In 1790, Revere made a new version of this copper plate by erasing the "Liberty Stump" imprint from the lower right hand corner of the plate.

[19] John Brooks was associated as of 2 March 1781 with Washington Lodge No. 10 chartered October 6, 1779, and with the American Union Lodge chartered 15 February 1776 as of 28 August 1779. Both were Army Lodges formed under the Grand Lodge of Massachusetts. Brooks was Master of Washington Lodge in 1781. See *Two Hundred and Fifty Years*, p. 24.

[20] Nathaniel Tracy was a Newburyport merchant. He had membership in St. John's Lodge, Newburyport in 1781, serving as Lodge Master in 1781–82. The Lodge was chartered 17 July 1766. According to masonic files, Tracy owned fifty privateers during the American Revolution. He died in 1796.

[21] This letter is owned by the Grand Lodge of Massachusetts A.F. & A.M., Archives. Although no specific Lodge is mentioned, Barrett signs his letter "Humble Servt + Brother," which suggests a masonic connection to Revere. It is not known for which Lodge the "jewels" might have been made, unless they were personal masonic jewels and not Lodge jewels. There is no reference in Revere's Wastebooks to jewels for this individual. The only "Jn Barrett" listed in the Grand Secretary's files is John Barrett, the first Master of Compass Lodge in Wallingsford, Connecticut, chartered 1 May 1769. It is not known whether this is the same man.

[22] Captain John Blanchard was initiated in Washington Lodge No. 10, an Army Lodge, on 8 December 1779. Active in the American Revolution, he served as a surgeon's mate. No copy of this certificate has been found. See Brigham, pp. 188–91.

[23] Dr. John Warren was a physician and surgeon during the Revolutionary War, and a brother of Joseph Warren. In 1780, he was a member of Massachusetts Lodge in Boston, chartered 13 May 1770. He was associated with St. Andrew's Lodge by 18 April 1777, and served as Grand Master of the Grand Lodge of Massachusetts for the years 1782–83 and 1787. See *Two Hundred and Fifty Years*, p. 45.

[24] Brigham, p. 191 connects this reference in the St. Andrew's Lodge Min-

utes to an existing notification made by Revere for St. Andrew's Lodge. A blank copy still survives. See Brigham, Plate 63 for photograph. Brigham also relates this notification to a reference in Revere's Rising States Lodge Record Book. This relationship is questionable. For explanation, see Note 26. There is no mention of the notification in Revere's Wastebook.

[25] King Solomon's Lodge was chartered in Charlestown on 5 September 1783.

[26] This item is included in the list only because Paul Revere may have made it, not because there is any definite evidence that he did. The reference is from Paul Revere's Rising States Lodge Record Book, owned by the Grand Lodge of Massachusetts A.F. & A.M., Archives. Revere used this book to keep accounts in 1784-85 while serving as the first Treasurer of Rising States Lodge, originally called St. Andrew's Lodge. Revere's entries begin in March 1784 under the name of St. Andrew's Lodge, and he continued to use this name through December, although the Lodge had voted to change its name to Rising States Lodge by 25 October 1784. The above reference indicates that the new St. Andrew's Lodge needed a "plate for summons." Although it seems likely that Revere would make a plate for his own Lodge, this reference does not necessarily prove that he did. Rather it only records the fact that, as Lodge Treasurer, he paid for the purchase of a plate. The plate is not mentioned in Revere's Wastebook. For the purposes of this list, the Rising States Lodge "copper plate" and the St. Andrew's Lodge notification (see 12 December 1784) have been considered as two distinctly different items, since they refer to separate Lodges. Brigham, p. 191, suggests that these are one and the same plate. While this is possible, confusion does result from the fact that both Lodges shared the same name (St. Andrew's) in early 1785 and it should not be assumed that the plate purchased by Rising States Lodge is necessarily the same plate owned by the Lodge of St. Andrew today. Despite the confusion, it is possible that in its early months the new St. Andrew's/Rising States Lodge did use a plate for summonses which bore the name of St. Andrew. On 25 October 1784, at the first meeting under the new name of Rising States Lodge, it was voted that "a Committee be Chose to furnish a Copper Plate for the Use of Summoning the Lodge together." From this reference, it seems that once the Lodge adopted a new name, it needed a new plate for the summonses. Since Paul Revere was among the three masons chosen for this committee, he would have been involved with procuring the plate. It can only be speculated whether or not he made it himself. The surviving Rising States Lodge minutes continue only until early 1785 and no further mention is made of the new plate. If Revere made a copper plate bearing the name of Rising States Lodge, it has not survived.

[27] This reference to jewels is also from Revere's Rising States Lodge Record Book. (See note 26.) Since the new Lodge, originally called St. Andrew's, was just forming in February 1784, Revere as Treasurer purchased many items for the Lodge in March, including the "Copper Plate" and Lodge jewels. Although it is possible that Revere made these jewels, there is no positive evidence that he did. The jewels have not survived. See the next item for reference to jewels in Revere's Wastebooks (Note 28). See Illustration 4 for the first page of Revere's Rising States Lodge Record Book, showing the many items he purchased for the new Lodge, including these jewels. Revere is also known to have made ladles and candlesticks for masonic use. Whether he made the "6 Ladles" or "3 p of Candlesticks" listed in the Record Book is also unknown.

[28] This item is from Revere's Wastebook. Revere did not record for which Lodge he made these jewels, but the date coincides with the purchase of

117

jewels for Rising States Lodge. It should be noted that the amounts charged in each instance do not coincide. See Note 27 for a discussion of Rising States Lodge jewels.

[29] Warren Lodge was chartered in Machias, Maine on 4 September 1778. James Avery became a member in the same year. He was also initiated into St. Andrew's Lodge on 27 February 1778. Avery served as Master of Warren Lodge in 1784, and as a Grand Lodge officer in 1783. According to Brigham, pp. 191–192, the reference to "Certificates" probably refers to the blank masonic certificates that Revere kept in his shop.

[30] The Grand Lodge of Massachusetts owns a seal for Rising States Lodge which it attributes to Revere with the date 1784. While the seal could be Revere's work, there is no mention of it in his Wastebook, nor is the purchase of a seal recorded in Revere's Rising States Lodge Record Book. For photograph of seal see Illustration 5.

[31] This could be Samuel Willis Hunt who was voted "to be made a Mason" in the Rising States Lodge Minutes, 25 October 1784. There was also a mason during this period named Samuel Wells Hunt, a Boston Custom House officer, who was a Grand Lodge officer in 1789 and a member of St. John's Lodge in 1790. The "Cross pens" may refer to the jewel for the office of Lodge Secretary, which consisted of two crossed quill pens.

[32] "Jenks" is probably John Jenks, who appears several times in Revere's Wastebooks. There are several John Jenkses in the files of the Grand Secretary. This could refer to the John Jenks who was an initiate in St. Andrew's Lodge on 13 November 1777. He also may be the same man who owned a Dry Goods Store at 39 State Street, Boston, in 1788. A John Jenks was also Secretary of Essex Lodge in Salem, at its founding. See *Proceedings* Vol. 2, p. 20 (8 June 1792).

[33] Brigham, p. 191, interprets this item as a sale of Revere's blank general masonic certificates. This customer is probably James Eveleth, the first Master of Lincoln Lodge, which was newly chartered on this day in Wiscasset, Maine. This is also the same James Eveleth who was initiated into St. Andrew's Lodge on 31 December 1777.

[34] The Columbian Lodge of Boston was chartered by Revere on 9 June 1796 while he was Grand Master of the Massachusetts Grand Lodge. According to the Grand Lodge *Proceedings* 1967, pp. 526, Revere made a set of ten jewels for Columbian Lodge which were melted down in 1810. There is no mention of these jewels in Revere's Wastebook. This receipt is owned by the Museum of Our National Heritage in Lexington, Massachusetts. See Illustration 9.

[35] Washington Lodge was chartered by Revere while he was Grand Master, on 17 March 1796. The Lodge, which was originally located in Roxbury, is now in Lexington. The jewels are still owned by the Lodge. There is no mention of these jewels in Revere's Wastebook. The jewels are dated to 1796 because one of the twelve jewels is engraved with the date "1796."

[36] According to Brigham, p. 191, in 1796, David Howe was Master of Hancock Lodge, located in Penobscot, Maine. This item probably refers to the sale of blank general certificates. David Howe was initiated into St. Andrew's Lodge on 30 April 1780, and voted with Paul Revere for the Massachusetts Grand Lodge in 1784. As of the meeting of 29 March 1784, Howe was a Senior Deacon of Rising States Lodge. He died in Castine, Maine in 1828.

[37] It is not known where this Lodge is located.

[38] According to Charles Messer Stow, p. 19, Samuel Dana was raised in St. Paul's Lodge on 27 February 1797. The Lodge was chartered by Revere while he was Grand Master on 26 January 1797. The Lodge was originally located in Groton, later moving to Ayer, Massachusetts.

[39] Seth Smith Jr. served as Master of Bristol Lodge in 1797–1798. The Lodge

was first located in Norton, later moving to N. Attleboro, Massachusetts. Paul Revere chartered Bristol Lodge while he was Grand Master on 14 June 1797. See Charles Messer Stow, p. 19.

[40] Paul Revere made a golden urn to preserve a lock of George Washington's hair which had been presented to the Grand Lodge in January 1800 by Washington's widow. The urn stands 3 ¾ inches tall and was later mounted on a mahogany pedestal which also doubles as a storage cabinet. See Illustration 8 and Section 10 of this work for a discussion of the urn and its inscription. A reference in the Grand Lodge minutes of 9 March 1801 indicates that the urn was not yet completed, as a "suitable inscription" was still being devised. This is the last reference to the golden urn in the Grand Lodge minutes. Assuming that the urn was completed sometime during 1801, the next reference in the minutes does not appear until 1812, when the mahogany case is first mentioned (*Proceedings* Vol. 2, p. 549, 14 December 1812). According to Martha Gandy Fales, the mahogany cabinet was probably made by Benjamin Frothingham, a cabinetmaker who knew Washington personally and was also a mason and a member of the Society of Cincinnati. Fales has no doubt that Revere made the urn. See Martha Gandy Fales, "The Golden Urn," paper in Paul Revere files, n.d., Grand Lodge of Massachusetts A.F. & A.M., Library, Boston, Massachusetts.

SELECTED BIBLIOGRAPHY

PRIMARY SOURCES: MANUSCRIPTS

Boston, Massachusetts. Grand Lodge of Massachusetts A.F. & A.M. Archives.
   Paul Revere Record Book 1784–1793, and Documents.
   Miscellaneous Masonic Correspondence and Documents.
   Rising States Lodge. Minutes of Meetings, 29 March 1784–28 February 1785.
Boston, Massachusetts. Grand Lodge of Massachusetts A.F. & A.M. Library.
   Lodge of St. Andrew. Minutes of Meetings, 1778–1854. Microfilm.
   Lodge of St. Andrew. Charters and Bylaws, 1760–1778, 1855–1872. Microfilm.
   Lodge of St. Andrew. Minutes of Masters Lodge Meetings, 1762–1802. Microfilm.
   Parker Index, 1733–1800.
Boston, Massachusetts. Lodge of St. Andrew. Minutes of Meetings, 1756–1778. Microfilm.
Boston, Massachusetts. Massachusetts Historical Society. Revere Family Papers.
   Account Ledger for the Workshop at Boston, 1761–1788.
   Cash Journal, 1785–1786.
   Loose Manuscripts, 1746–1801.
   Waste and Memoranda Books for the Workshop at Boston, 1761–1783, 1783–1797.
"Masonic Funeral Solemnities." (Portsmouth N.H.) *The United States Oracle of the Day*, 22 February 1800.

PRINTED PRIMARY SOURCES

Bentley, William. *The Diary of William Bentley, D.D. Pastor of the East Church, Salem, Massachusetts.* 2 vols. Salem, Massachusetts: The Essex Institute, 1905–1907.
Celebration of the One-Hundred and Twenty-Fifth Anniversary of St. Andrew's Royal Arch Chapter 1769–1894. Boston: Published by the Chapter, Printers S.J. Parkhill and Company, 1894.
Centennial Memorial of the Lodge of St. Andrew. Boston: Printed by vote of the Lodge of St. Andrew, 1870.
Commemoration of the One Hundred and Fiftieth Anniversary of the Lodge of St.

Andrew 1756–1906. Boston: Printed by vote of the Lodge of St. Andrew by the Riverside Press, Cambridge, Massachusetts, 1907.

The Constitutions of the Ancient and Honorable Fraternity of Free and Accepted Masons: Containing their History, Charges, Addresses and Collected and Digested from Their Old Records, Faithful Traditions and Lodge Books. For The Use of Masons To Which are added The History of Masonry in the Commonwealth of Massachusetts, and the Constitution, Laws and Regulations of Their Grand Lodge together with a Large Collection of Songs, Epilogues, etc. Worcester, Massachusetts: Published by the Massachusetts Grand Lodge, Printed by Isaiah Thomas, 1792.

Crocker, Hannah Mather. *A Series of Letters on Freemasonry by a Lady of Boston.* Boston: Printed by John Eliot, 1815.

Gurley, John Ward. *An Address on the Origin and Principles of Freemasonry.* Boston: Printed by Brothers Russell and Cutler for St. John's Lodge, 1800.

Harris, Thaddeus Mason. *Masonic Emblems Explained.* Boston: Printed by William Spotswood for the subscribers, July 1796.

History of St. John's Lodge of Boston. Boston: privately printed, 1917.

Paul Revere's Three Accounts of His Famous Ride. Portland, Maine: Anthoesen Press, 1968.

Proceedings in Masonry. St. John's Grand Lodge 1733–1792 Massachusetts Grand Lodge 1769–1792. Boston: Published by the Grand Lodge of Massachusetts, Press of Rockwell and Churchill, 1895.

Proceedings of the Most Worshipful Grand Lodge of Ancient Free and Accepted Masons of the Commonwealth of Massachusetts in Union with the Most Ancient and Honorable Grand Lodge in Europe and America, According to the Old Constitutions 1792–1815. Cambridge: Press of Caustic-Claflin Company, 1905.

SECONDARY SOURCES

Ammerman, David. *In the Common Cause: American Response to the Coercive Acts of 1774.* New York: W.W. Norton and Company, Inc., 1974.

Boston, Massachusetts. Grand Lodge of Massachusetts A.F. & A.M. Library. Paul Revere Files.

Boston, Massachusetts. Grand Lodge of Massachusetts A.F. & A.M. Office of the Grand Secretary. Membership Files.

Boston, Massachusetts. Paul Revere House Library. "Paul Revere Papers." Inventory of the Revere Papers at the Massachusetts Historical Society with a Compilation of Data 1770–1800. (Typewritten).

Brigham, Clarence C. *Paul Revere's Engravings.* New York: Atheneum, 1969.

Buhler, Kathryn C. *Paul Revere Goldsmith 1735–1818.* Boston, Massachusetts: Museum of Fine Arts, n.d.

Carr, Harry. *Six Hundred Years of Craft Ritual.* Grand Lodge of Missouri, 1977.

Cassidy, Matthew and Webster, Linda. "Paul Revere, An Officer and a Gentleman: The Penobscot Campaign of 1779." Boston, 1983.

Ely, Carol. "North Square: A Boston Neighborhood in the Revolutionary Era." Boston, March 1983.

Fales, Martha Gandy. "The Golden Urn." Paper in Paul Revere Files. Grand Lodge of Massachusetts A.F. & A.M. Library. Boston, Massachusetts. (Typewritten).

Flynt, Henry N. and Fales, Martha Gandy. *The Heritage Foundation Collection of Silver with Biographical Sketches of New England Silversmiths 1625–1825*. Old Deerfield, Massachusetts: The Heritage Foundation, 1968.

Forbes, Esther. *Paul Revere and the World He Lived In*. Boston: Houghton Mifflin Company, 1942.

Friedman, Ruth L. "Artisan to Entrepreneur: The Business Life of Paul Revere." Boston, Spring 1978.

Goss, Elbridge Henry. *The Life of Colonel Paul Revere*. 2 vols. Boston: Joseph George Cupples, 1891.

Grand Lodge of Masons in Massachusetts. *Two Hundred and Fifty Years of Massachusetts Masonry*. Boston: Rapid Service Press, 1983.

Jones, Mervyn. "Freemasonry." In Mackenzie, Norman, ed. *Secret Societies*. New York: Crescent Books, Inc., 1967, pp. 152–178.

Kemper, Elmer T. "Hiram, King of Tyre 'Pillar of Strength.'" *California Freemason* (Summer 1973).

King, Louis C. "The Grand Lodge of Massachusetts Birthplace of Freemasonry." *Trowel* 1 (April 1983): 4–7.

Kutolowski, Kathleen Smith. "Freemasonry and Community in the Early Republic: The Case For Antimasonic Anxieties." *American Quarterly* 34 (Winter 1982): 543–61.

Lipson, Dorothy Ann. *Freemasonry in Federalist Connecticut 1789–1832*. Princeton: Princeton University Press, 1977.

Most Worshipful Grand Lodge of Ancient Free and Accepted Masons of the Commonwealth of Massachusetts Directory, 1981.

Parker, Henry J. *Army Lodges During the Revolution*. Boston, 1884.

Pollard, Ralph J. *Famous American Freemasons*. Silver Spring, Maryland: Masonic Service Association, 15 October 1971.

Roberts, Allen E. *The Craft and Its Symbols: Opening the Door to Masonic Symbolism*. Richmond, Virginia: Macoy Publishing and Masonic Supply Company, Inc., 1974.

Stow, Charles Messer. "Paul Revere, Craftsman." *Transactions of the American Lodge of Research, Free and Accepted Masons*. New York: Grand Lodge of Free and Accepted Masons, State of New York. 5 (18 December 1947–31 May 1949): 13–20.

Tatsch, J. Hugo. *Freemasonry in the Thirteen Colonies*. New York: Macoy Publishing and Masonic Supply Company, 1929.

Taylor, Earl W. *Historical Sketch of the Grand Lodge of Masons in Massachusetts From Its Beginnings in 1733 To The Present Time*. Boston, Massachusetts: Grand Lodge of Masons in Massachusetts, 1973.

Vaughn, William Preston. *The Anti-Masonic Party in the United States 1826–1843*. Lexington, Kentucky: The University of Kentucky Press, 1983.

Whitehill, Walter Muir. *Boston, A Topographical History*. Cambridge, Massachusetts: The Belknap Press of Harvard University Press, 1959.

A2 113
7½-12